BRAVELY YOU, BRAVELY ME

BEING YOU WITHOUT APOLOGY

CHIRON O'KEEFE

Copyright © 2019 by Chiron O'Keefe

Published in Portland, Oregon, United States

All rights reserved.

No part of this book may be reproduced in any form or by any electronic or mechanical means, including information storage and retrieval systems, without written permission from the author, except for the use of brief quotations in a book review.

Library of Congress Control Number 2019909905

ISBN 978-1-7331758-0-7 (trade paperback)

ISBN 978-1-7331758-1-4 (eBook)

To Wendy and Shawn and all those who became Me

CONTENTS

Preface	vii

PART ONE

1. A Star Dreams	3
2. In the Beginning	5
3. Surfing on a Sea of Trust	15
4. Marbles of Wisdom	23
5. The Universe Whispers, "Remember"	29
6. To Expect or Not Expect, That is the Question	35
7. No is a Complete Sentence	46

PART TWO

8. The Question of Me	61
9. Bravely Me	65
10. The New Normal	79
11. Who Do I Think I Am?	90
12. Creating a New Backstory	97
13. Be True To Your Self	106

PART THREE

14. Life Sculptors	131
15. Putting My Past in Front of Me	133
16. Embracing The Discomfort Zone	146
17. Pushing Against A Wall	154
18. Remembering the Magic	159
19. Funhouse Mirror Effect	170
20. Our Future Beckons	183
21. Our Heroic Self	185

PART FOUR

22. Without Apology	193
23. We Must Be The Heroes We Seek	196
24. Our Choices Define Us	202
25. Our Lens of Reality	209
26. Choosing Our Beliefs	219

PART FIVE

27. Here is Where We'll Meet	231
28. I Am Amazing because...	233
29. Fall In Love With Yourself	237
30. The Unfinished Portrait	247
31. Our Way Home	251
Acknowledgments	255
About the Author	257

PREFACE

The good news is, no one ever found anything truly amazing without searching. It is the lost who wander, and only the wanderers discover new shores.
— Dr. Salma Farook, *What Your Soul Already Knows.*

Every soul starts life the same way, with a triumphant, sometimes traumatic process of physical birth our conscious mind cannot recall. Our childhood, family dynamics, and earliest friendships are like a sculptor's chisel, carving out a personality and a set of beliefs that may seem set in stone. For some, the early years leave us feeling as if the chisel slipped. Instead of smooth marble and transcendent beauty, we view only vivid scars in the rock, sharp and jagged chips of memory that continue to cut painfully.

When the agony of early years overwhelms, we tend to recall only those fragments of events that support our misery. A belief of being unattractive may push me to remember quite vividly the time Ellen M. called out to me in seventh grade as I strolled past the lockers. Self-consciously squinting in my nearsighted world, I could barely see her face but her aggressive energy could be felt even from a distance.

"Hey, doesn't your mother sell Vanda Beauty Counselor make-up?"

A rival to Avon products back in the sixties, VBC offered a wide range of products that housewives could hawk to earn extra cash. My mom dabbled with selling while still holding down one and sometimes two waitressing jobs.

I nodded with hesitation. Ellen had an unpleasant edge and regularly looked down her nose or pointedly ignored me. Why was she talking to me now?

"Isn't make-up supposed to make you look pretty?"

Again, I nodded, uncertain and wary.

"Then why don't you wear some?" She immediately burst into shrill laughter, echoed with cruel glee by her followers.

While this wasn't an earth-shattering moment, it certainly stung and had a long-term impact on my self-perception. It reinforced my hidden fear that I was unlovable. My shame amplified every time I dredged up this unpleasant memory, supporting the miserable belief that my unattractiveness horrified others and was indeed something to be embarrassed about.

This is an automatic process of reinforcement we all do on an ongoing basis. We forget the scattered bits of pleasure, shimmering like polished stones on a river bank, urging us to recall the brilliant moments of delight we all require to survive and thrive in life. We depend on inspiration from ourselves or others to sustain us when we forget. We must dig deeply within to regain our curiosity, confidence, and courage.

Every being learns to live in the same manner as a toddler learns to walk. Struggling to first rise up on our own two legs with tentative resolve, and eventually learning to balance with bold assurance.

Who am I?

The unspoken question poses our greatest challenge.

The following chapters are my own exploration of this very question.

They are deeply personal, a blend of gentle reminders to myself, along with those that probe deeper—an occasionally raw, uncensored scrutiny of my psyche I offer up, trusting others on a similar journey may find insight.

This is my message to you.

No matter what tragedy you've endured, despite the horrendous challenges and overwhelming opposition that crumpled your soul, you can learn to become *you* without restraint, without hesitation. You have the capacity to break through the limits others have imposed, tear off the chains of obligation and guilt from years of conditioning or abuse, and reach deep within to discover who you are. Even better, to reveal who you yearn to become.

You have the power within you. You have had this power all along. It is now time to embrace your potential to live deeply and honestly. It is your destiny to discover and become the best possible version of yourself.

The first chapter reveals a glimpse of my early years. I draw back the shades to offer perspective of my own journey.

Beginning with Chapter Three, there will be a suggested focus, affirmation, and follow-up review at the end of each chapter. These are tools designed to inspire you to dig deeper, to examine and explore your feelings, and to form a more intimate relationship with your soul. It is recommended that you utilize a notebook dedicated for use with these exercises so that you can record each insight and every reveal that arises.

In Heinlein's science-fiction masterpiece, *Stranger in a Strange Land*, he coined the term grok. The word was meant to convey an understanding so complete we become one with what we are observing or knowing. "May you drink deeply," meaning "to drink in all available aspects of reality." This is our ultimate goal in life. To understand ourselves so beautifully, that we can flow into a sense of ease and trust—to grasp how to fully, confidently, and exuberantly be our most authentic self.

To truly master an understanding of a situation, and of life itself, we circle back time and time again. Many of the ideas introduced will be revisited in subsequent chapters, explored in more depth or from a different angle. To gain perspective, we must develop an understanding that burrows beneath the surface and expands into a holistic comprehension.

The purpose of this book is to inspire and encourage you towards a life of authenticity, accountability, and grace. The exercises provided can assist in gently uncovering those jagged edges that still jab at the soul. Without awareness to provide strength and understanding, we may adopt coping mechanisms to provide cover, only to find the fabric of compensating beliefs snags on those unacknowledged broken bits of self. The purpose here is to teach you how to utilize insights and newfound awareness to rebuild the fragmented psyche shattered by early experiences, and discover the Self behind the many masks you felt obligated to wear. Stripping away the habits of mind to reveal our beliefs and embracing the sometimes painful challenge of being accountable for our choices (whether those choices are deliberate or unconscious) is our path to successful self-transformation.

Let's begin our journey together.

The stories in this book reflect the author's recollection of events. Some names and identifying characteristics have been changed to protect the privacy of those depicted. Dialogue has been re-created from memory.

PART ONE

SELF-CONSCIOUS: WHO AM I?

ONE
A STAR DREAMS

A molecule breathes,
yearns for dreams
of laughter,
of lights so bright
a star
would stare in wonder.

A molecule dreams
within a breath,
a starry dance of
dandelion kisses that float
gently in the sky.

A puff of breath
and my dreams
dance
within each molecule.

Whose hand
will pluck me
from my eternal sky?

TWO
IN THE BEGINNING

There is no place like home.

L. FRANK BAUM, *THE WONDERFUL WIZARD OF OZ*

A child needs love.

Being cared for is not just a biological necessity. Without nurturing, a soul fails to thrive. A devastating study in the 1960s by Harry Harlow forcibly separated infant monkeys from their mothers, detailing the stark horrific results of emotional neglect.

Sitting in class, I squirmed in my seat as the film dispassionately displayed a cruelty that would haunt me. The implications were meant to be a learning tool, to help students studying childhood development gain objective understanding.

Viewing quaking, desperate beings crying out for mothers they would never be allowed to touch was torturous. Who could possibly view this objectively?

Not me.

The fearfulness, the horror of being raised without nurturing echoed my own background too well.

I was a child who desperately needed a loving home.

My childhood was ripped apart by the abrupt death of my father at age thirty-six. This left us stranded with a shell-shocked, bitter mother whose immediate response was to mercilessly ship us off to the opposite coast to live with our paternal grandparents for close to a year. When we were finally allowed to return home, our mother's visible resentment baffled us all. Neither love nor comfort was offered. Sometimes tragedy brings a family together. They bond over their shared grief, taking solace in the love that remains. My mom was too broken inside to see us as individuals, as children who needed nurturing and a home.

This is when I first discovered words could be used not only to awaken a curious mind or heal a tender heart—bitter words could also be hurled with careless intent, shattering a vulnerable psyche.

"I never wanted kids. It was your father who wanted children, and then he died, leaving me stuck with you."

*"I wish **you** had died instead of your father."*

This was a message repeated throughout the decades of my life. A stark, horrifying truth to a child's mind. We were unwanted, unloved burdens. So there I was, fatherless and metaphorically motherless at age three, leading to a numbing pattern of being neglected or abused by various caretakers.

Unlike the terrified monkeys cruelly tortured for what struck me as a sadistic purpose, there was one path of solace for me.

Reading.

The same mom who never cuddled, or comforted, or hugged, encouraged me to read. She signed us up for a children's Book of the Month club. One day a box arrived and she called me over. With a happy grin, she slit open the packing tape to reveal a treasure. Inside lay the complete series of Oz books by L. Frank Baum that begins with *The Wonderful Wizard of Oz*.

You have plenty of courage, I am sure," answered Oz. "All you need is confidence in yourself. There is no living thing that is not afraid when it faces danger. The true courage is in facing danger when you are afraid, and that kind of courage you have in plenty.

L. FRANK BAUM

Books would provide a shelter for my loneliness. Characters became imaginary friends. At age ten, I relished my adventures in Oz. In one book, a fascinating tidbit informed how Glinda the Good's magical book recorded every action taken, every word spoken. My desperation to be whisked away like Dorothy burned inside me. Crawling out of my bedroom window, I scrambled up onto the roof of my stepfather's house.

"Please, Glinda! I want to go to Oz!" I whispered feverishly.

Sometimes it's easier to believe in fairy tales than real life. If I just focused hard enough, would the Wonderful Wizard use Ozma's magic picture to pinpoint my location and work with Glinda the Good to whisk me away? Would they bring me... home?

Despite her failings in nurturing, Mom was a character—smart, funny, and determined to be herself. In later years, we'd grow closer, bonding mostly over our shared passion for books. I learned to recognize that there were lasting benefits paired with the intense challenges of my early years. Oh, but those challenges.

We moved constantly, struggling with the stigma and anxiety of being fatherless and barely mothered. Mom always had some issue or another that could only be resolved by scooping up stuff off the floor, tossing it into boxes, and heading to yet another rental.

Within a few months of moving to Crestline, California, she met a guy in a bar and brought him home. Innocently barging into my mom's bedroom was a shock. So I first met Ray one morning when he was naked in my mother's bed. I was eight years old at the time

Four years after my dad's death, she married this raging alcoholic who terrified and abused us all.

Nights would be filled with screams, days overwrought with trepidation. Like a soldier in combat, we never knew when the enemy would strike. An innocent word could trigger an explosive rage. Decades later, I recognize there are still traces of PTSD wired into my brain from my earliest years.

Sleeping peacefully, only to be yanked out of dreams by the screams of my mother. Crawling out of bed to watch in horrified silence as Ray threw her to the ground, kicking her ribs with steel-toed boots. Calling her a whore, a bitch.

"Call the police, Jeff!" she'd scream to my older, teenage brother somewhere off in the house. Whether he did or not, I'll never know. The police never arrived. Mom would cover up her bruises the next day and tell us to mind our own business.

Ray was a brute. He'd come home stinking of alcohol with a mean, ugly look of warning carved into his face—just looking for trouble. If I dared to look his way when he was in a mood, the ferocity of his slap would knock me to the floor. I would lay there, shivering with fear. Like prey terrorized by a wild predator, I'd lay motionless silently praying his hunger would be sated by my compliance.

He loved to humiliate. Forcing me at age ten to remove my shirt and sit outside to 'teach me a lesson.' The mountain air was chilly enough to raise goose bumps on my skinny arms. When neighbors walked by, they'd look away while my face burned with feverish shame.

The chaos encountered left me chronically bewildered and anxious.

Mom would angrily throw clothes in suitcases, and we'd flee Ray's home, only to return again and again. We finally moved out for the final time, furniture abandoned and with nothing but my beloved cat and whatever belongings could be shoved haphazardly into the station wagon.

My brother had run away at age seventeen to join the navy. I felt nothing but relief. He was broken too. His rage mimicked our stepfather. It was safer without him near.

Which left only my sister and me, crammed with mom into one room at the motel for our last night in Crestline. Mom tells me, "We only had enough money to grab dinner but your sister insisted on using the last ten dollars to go to a concert." As if her eldest daughter was somehow to blame for her own lack of priorities, her own inability to exert control.

The unspoken message was clear.

My sister insisted on having her desires fulfilled, her needs met. Therefore *she* was selfish. A good girl takes what she's given without complaint. A terrible lesson which would fester within me for years to come until I'd learned enough to break free of the self-imposed chains of guilt and obligation.

So Mom and I hunkered down that night in a cramped motel room, spooning up Campbell's Bean with Bacon soup heated in an electric skillet precariously perched on a rickety dresser. Waiting to move to Sunset Beach where we'd begin yet again. Shortly after, my sister's destructive tendencies overloaded. Jabbing her arm bloody with a rattail comb while incarcerated in juvenile detention, she was transferred to Camarillo State Mental Hospital where she would reside until age eighteen.

At age twelve, I was for all purposes now an only child with a mom who expected me to nurture and care for myself. A few months earlier, I'd shamefacedly asked her if I could use her deodorant. She laughed and said I was too young to need it.

Apparently she never smelt the rank odor of stark fear that permeated my body.

It's odd to recognize in retrospect how I was bombarded by a nearly constant sense of anxiety from which there was no realistic escape. Except by crawling between the tattered covers of my favorite books.

Dorothy of Oz became my first inspirational hero.

The movie changed the meaning, supposing instead our heroine dreamt up the whole scenario as a psychological tale to work through her anger and fear. Not a bad twist, but I preferred the real story.

In the book, those magic shoes whisked Dorothy across the deadly desert to return her safely home to Uncle Henry and Aunt Em. The message was more than, "There's no place like home." It also stated quite firmly that magic is real and adventures can happen in the blink of an eye.

The death of my father and the chaotic spiral of tragedy that tore apart my home, threw me into a tornado of circumstances over which I would have no hope of control. Yet I learned to survive and even thrive, just as my mythic hero did. Not content to dismiss my past as a nightmare, I learned to recognize how we encounter circumstances designed to teach us to wake up from any self-imposed illusions. A dream can't come true unless you recognize the magic within your own choices.

Our truest purpose in life is to explore and develop our own set of values. We all must face challenges, sometimes seemingly impossible quests. Instinctively, I grasped there truly is no place like home. However, the idea of home is more than a domicile with four walls and a roof. We carry our own sense of home within our hearts, within our souls. It's why some newfound friends feel like long-lost sisters or brothers. It's also why when we gain a sense of who we yearn to be, beyond the insistent demands of others, beyond the impositions of society or a job or artificially adopted expectations, we feel a sense of finally making our way home.

For me, and for others, outer circumstances may feel beyond our control, but it's always the inner choices we make that save us.

Like Dorothy, I needed to understand myself, to discover and transform into the person that my inner self yearned to be. Inspired by my first mythical hero, my unconscious goal was to become a hero with honor and integrity. To experience life through a mind that believed in magic.

The outside world I experienced had no heroes available, yet my inner life, rich with the colorful adventures within fictional tales, provided a secure psychological background and a rather intriguing dynamic. Over the years, it became increasingly clear that stories offered substitute worlds and transferring myself *there,* even just imaginatively, would strengthen me. I developed resiliency by balancing the outer physical world and my inner life, ripe with those vivid stories of wonder and magic.

It is within those tales that I learned to recognize how a spectacular quest can begin in the blink of an eye. A person can be strolling down an ordinary lane in one moment, and then suddenly discover it's the magical Road to Oz. Without thinking we might scoop up a worn nickel nestled within a crack in the sidewalk. Soon it becomes clear this is a magic coin opening the door to a thrilling adventure, along with a few hard-earned but well-appreciated lessons.

My background could indeed have wrung all the color out of my soul, yet instead I let the whirlwind of circumstances force me into a quest of self-discovery. Like the Tin Woodman, my heart would open and I'd learn to let hidden tears spill out without fear of being immobilized by rusty emotions too long repressed. My desire for a brain would be sated by old-fashioned study of endless books, the truest magic I've encountered. Courage would be the toughest lesson of all, yet if the Cowardly Lion could face down his own fears, why couldn't I?

The world is composed of stories we create.

We learn to read by memorizing letters, sounds, and then spelling out words. Yet how is it that we learn how to live? Teaching a child only to memorize facts may make him a good student. Encourage a child to read for pleasure, and she'll master a variety of subjects just to satiate a burning hunger for knowledge and awareness. Even better, she'll develop the capacity to reason, to be simultaneously receptive and skeptical. The ability to weigh equally the practical and the fanciful is the secret every hero learns.

The Imaginative Child will become the imaginative man or woman most apt to create, to invent, and therefore to foster civilization.

L. FRANK BAUM

However it isn't the books that teach us; books only provide a framework for understanding. We learn by doing, by experiencing life, and examining our experiences through a heroic perspective. The ultimate goal: to recognize we are all heroes of our own tales.

We must recognize that each tragedy and every heartbreak teaches us. Seeking out the wisdom even in moments that shatter us is as vital as relishing the moments of delight that lift our hearts. We learn by paying attention and seeking out those intense, invaluable insights, for they are always there just waiting for us to notice.

This is the path I have chosen, the path I wish to share with you.

It's up to us to embrace destiny and recognize our role as the storytellers of our lives. We must seek out and share tales of our own wonder and self-discovery. Our shared stories, along with the hopes we confide can create an unquenchable yearning for a sparkling world of innovation and progress. This is how we will change our world collectively. This is also how you and I can change our personal reality.

We need to become our own heroes.

If we ever get a chance to meet, here's what I yearn to hear: tell me *your* favorite stories. The names of those worn and tattered books that changed your life. Share with me the dazzling tales that stirred up insatiable hunger only more fables could satisfy. Let's help each other to remember. Those precious stories are luminous lighthouses we can use to safely guide us to shore, to remind us of who we are, deep within our souls. Then we can recognize how we are constantly writing and rewriting the ongoing story of life. At some point, many of us may lose the faith we all carried instinctively; the trust that allows a frisky squirrel to leap from branch to branch or a fragrant rose to reach for the sky.

For decades, I yearned to compose fictional sagas of wonder and magic. Instead, my heart guided me to pen a different sort of tale, to recognize the ongoing story woven throughout each dawning hour of my life. My heart listened to the searching questions springing from the hearts of other seekers. Questions that echoed my own constant desire to find meaning within my life, and to discover exactly who I might be.

To know and become myself is the goal. To explore and discern the me of me, the seed buried deep under a pile of circumstances thick enough to block the sun.

My quest for self-understanding mingled with my desire to help others piece together their own life puzzle. Often, I would find myself responding to another's heart-cry with an essay. Realizing, even as I typed, any answers springing from deep within my soul were not meant just for me.

Within these covers, I share my personal writings. These are thoughts explored and collected throughout the years. My intent is for you to find value, solace, illumination, and comfort for internal aches not yet acknowledged. Life can seem like a struggle when we forget that it has purpose. Each lesson provides value, and through each challenge successfully met, we discover more of our potential. Our lifelong quest is to explore, discover and eventually become our Selves. This ongoing tale of self-discovery filled with novel experiences and intimate revelations is our own mystical saga.

It is now time to remember the inherent magic within your soul. Your life is filled with inexplicable beauty and immense power, and the most potent tool for transformation will be to reclaim the childlike trust that is your birthright.

THREE
SURFING ON A SEA OF TRUST

To have faith is to trust yourself to the water. When you swim you don't grab hold of the water, because if you do you will sink and drown. Instead you relax, and float.

ALAN WATTS

Many a powerful being shares a common theme in their earliest years. Challenging situations (to put it mildly) threaten to shatter them into a billion pieces, yet ultimately end up teaching lessons that endure throughout life. Some budding souls were terrified by edgy chaos or cowed by those whom, in their ignorance, heartlessly bullied fragile selves. Many felt demoralized by oppressive circumstances or simply heartbroken by distracted caretakers offering meager sustenance and even less warmth or affection.

To a child of tender years, it boils down to *circumstances seemingly beyond our control.*

Despite the inevitable terror and nail-biting anxiety

resulting from being raised in a household that was at times cruelly abusive and other times simply neglectful (yet always precarious), I somehow emerged with heart and mind intact. At age seven, the universe provided me with a beautiful opportunity, a lesson in trust.

I was a small, skinny child with little supervision and no close friends. In the sixties, Sunset Beach and Surfside were tiny, nearly identical, beach towns along the Pacific Coast Highway in Southern California. The seasons blurred together, smudged by a perpetual summer heat where tanned surfers with hair bleached white and eyes as blue as an eternal sky would be toting surfboards 365 days a year.

My father's death was three years behind us. Mom needed to work so she found a small apartment near the restaurant owned by her eldest sibling, Fran. Noel's Cafe, a seafood dinner spot smack dab on the Pacific Coast Highway, was a small and funky eatery with the wildest decorations a kid could imagine. A mammoth lobster adorned one wall, a gigantic sea turtle hung on another. A shiny black diving suit with teensy colored lights in the helmet stood in one corner, hanging basket-chairs in another, and a puffer fish glowed with eerie magnificence near the entrance.

Aunt Fran had written her own homily on a scallop-edged placemat, framed and hanging over the hostess station: *This ain't the Ritz. No fancy linen, no tablecloths, just good food and fast service.*

During the day Mom spent her free time hanging out with Fran, hours before she'd begin taking orders and hustling out heaping plates of deep-fried sea scallops, crunchy shrimp, steamed crab legs and lobster to an endless stream of hungry customers. Mom preferred the company of adults over children, and my older siblings couldn't be bothered to watch over me, which meant I was left on my own and free to roam. The tiny strip towns were nestled between the Pacific Coast Highway, known fondly as PCH, and the favored playground—our local beach, comprised of blistering hot sand and cool ocean waves.

What child could resist the lure of the ocean?

The sea became one of my earliest teachers.

The frothy blue-green waves fascinated me. I'd stroll up and down, leaving footprints in the damp sand. However there was a distinct challenge. In between where the waves crash on the shore and the churning ocean lay a hidden chasm. A sucking maw that you could hear faintly. One...two...three steps and down you went. It was an either/or situation. You walked and then had to make this leap of faith to get past the drop-off. That was the first challenge.

The second challenge would be to learn how to bodysurf—turning into a mythical sea-creature, at least in my imagination. This is how the Pacific Ocean became one of my first teachers. Her gift to me was wrapped up in the potential for perhaps the most fun I could imagine.

The promised reward—the thrill of delicious moments soaring on the waves like a frisky dolphin. The hidden gift—a potent lesson.

I formed a relationship with the ocean. Our time together transformed my child-like perspective. The lessons in trust would empower me, even without conscious awareness of what exactly I was learning.

Some perceive the sea as a wild, untamed creature, an ancient monster that requires no mythological serpents to destroy seafaring vessels. Yet there is rhythm and solace in those crashing waves. Children perceive nature with an unbiased eye. We feel a kinship too many of us forget as the years pile on. In those early years, we inexplicably know leafy trees cradle our searching limbs, the gentle wind lovingly caresses our cheeks, vibrant raindrops form puddle-playgrounds welcoming our exuberant splashing play, and the shimmering ocean is a vast consciousness as wise and potent as the Earth herself.

At age seven, edging closer to the sea, the dry hot sand transformed into damp coolness for my appreciative toes. I'd venture forth and completely surrender my fears and my self to the vast churning waters beckoning. Often my floundering attempts resulted not in the delicious thrill of catching a soaring wave. Nope, instead, like a frisky feline chasing an insubstantial ball of fluff, the wave caught *me*.

With watery fingers she'd raise me high enough to taste the burning sun right before powerfully flinging me deep underwater. Plunging down, I'd haphazardly tumble without a speck of control, scraping painfully against the sandy floor. Seemingly so close to the surface and yet so far from the oxygen every human desperately requires to live.

Each time I'd feel myself questioning: *Is this it? Is this where I die?*

My thoughts weren't always verbalized. What I distinctly remember was a noticeable lack of panic and my complete, unquestioned acceptance. Tumbling in the water, hovering in a state of uncertainty, I was aware of the fragility within every moment. Yes, indeed, I might succumb to the watery depths but I felt absolutely no fear.

Crazy, I know.

Perhaps being so young meant I still retained the faintest memory of other lives. An awareness of existence beyond mortality hovered closer to my consciousness than it would later, many years down the line.

But children know what adults soon forget.

We sense mortal life and the mystery of death are inexplicably entwined. Death is not yet feared for we haven't been trained yet to believe in mortality.

Is this it?

Spinning, tumbling, having no choice but to relinquish all control, trusting—then as the mighty ocean graciously withdrew her tight grip, I'd claw my way up, breaking through the watery surface to gulp a lungful of sweet and salty air: exultant I had survived, yet again.

In retrospect, perhaps it was the combination of delicious fun and an absolute requirement of unwavering trust that formed the basis of this unique relationship. All I know is we bonded; this wild, ephemeral being called to me. She benevolently taught me to release and surrender, to recognize the futility of fear, to know that trust would always be my surest and most reliable guide.

As days progressed into years, this powerful lesson would resurface repeatedly. Just as I had triumphantly risen from those watery depths, so would I rise again when an ocean of painful or fearful circumstances might appear overwhelming. I could trust there is always a still and secure presence of mind to guide me; a consciousness within the universe willing to teach me whatever lesson might serve my growth. This potent awareness is available to all of us. Trust can and will guide us no matter how ferocious, fearsome, or precarious circumstances appear to be. Trust will reveal how to break through and gratefully breathe in a solution to bring us sparkling hope and true clarity. Trust will always teach us how to gracefully rise above and surf those magnificent waves.

SUGGESTED FOCUS:

Think of a fun activity you believe to be challenging. It could be an activity you already explore or a choice outside of your comfort zone. Sky-diving or cartwheels, dancing or meditating, public speaking or one-on-one conversations, planting a garden or painting, singing a song or stretching into a yogic pose, or even surfing those magnificent waves.

Choose your focus. Imagine yourself within your activity. Visualize a larger presence guiding you. For some this presence may be thought of as God, or a universal consciousness, yet within that is an extension of your own self, a greater you working within this universal consciousness. A self who is outside of the boundaries of time and space. Your whole self perceives your life beyond the daily footprint of linear time, sees every day from birth on, and lovingly guides from a perspective of total awareness. You are the portion of your whole self that exists within this physical framework. Your whole self cradles you with love.

Envision Fun! Picture yourself leaping into the unknown and feeling the trust of being guided by this larger portion of self. Let yourself dwell in this focus until you feel the connection.

AFFIRMATION: I float on a sea of trust.

REVIEW:

In your notebook, record your chosen focus and explore the feelings that arise. Did you feel excited, nervous, skeptical, hopeful, or what? Could you imagine yourself successfully going through with your activity? If not, let's explore the feelings that surfaced.

Imagine the You who is journaling now has the opportunity to help the you within the imaginative exercise. Visualize yourself stepping in and offering assistance.

If you're visualizing an art project, imagine seeing yourself as a larger presence, guiding your hand. If it's a physical activity, such as rock-climbing or skydiving, again strive to imagine you *are viewing the scene from outside your physical body and whisper enthusiastic encouragement to the self taking on the challenge. Allow yourself to feel the connection between you, the physical self living day to day, and your whole self who perceives your entire life from a larger perspective.*

Within physical life, we often rely only on our physical senses and personal memories, yet we are much more.

The idea of reincarnation is woven into the fabric of many ancient cultures, as well as being the central tenet for all major Indian religions, such as Hinduism, Buddhism, Sikhism, and Jainism. Pythagoras, Socrates, and Plato, the noted philosophers in historical Greece, embraced this belief in rebirth or metempsychosis. The idea that the soul is immortal has been in existence for eons.

Many speak of a "higher self" yet in my view the self expands outward like a spiral, growing more aware of its identity.

In the book Seth Speaks, Seth speaking through Jane Roberts summed it up perfectly:

"Development unfolds in all directions. The soul is not ascending a series of stairs, each one representing a new and higher point of development.

Instead, the soul stands at the center of itself, exploring, extending its capacities in all directions at once, involved in issues of creativity, each one highly legitimate."

Like many others, I have come to realize that my full being is not limited to the physical plane. Carl Jung spoke of a "collective consciousness" which may be consciously accessed through our intuition. Our current physical focus could be likened to a dream of our larger identity: an ongoing story within the physical plane. When we fall asleep, we may meet up with other aspects of our larger identity, which I often simply term my Self. We often can access wisdom, insight, understanding, and even flashes of intuition from our greater Selves.

For those who (like me) believe the soul continues to incarnate through many lives, our greater Self would be the larger identity who is aware of all incarnations; who remembers most clearly the lessons and intent as each personality is born into a new life; who lovingly offers insight, support, and wisdom throughout the process of learning within the physical framework.

Transcendentalism utilized the term Oversoul, to describe this larger identity that is both the greater Me (who may be perceived as an unseen guide), and the personal, physical, boots-on-the-ground me who is traipsing through life, piecing together and achieving awareness one day, one life at a time. Fairy tales spoke of Fairy Godmothers, and some cultures speak of the Great Spirit or God. The feeling can be both intimate and universal.

We can all access that spark of divine energy within us. Whether we call it a guide, an oversoul, spirit, or our larger identity. The more we practice tuning into that essence and taking on that mantle of wise intuition, the easier it gets.

Write a note to yourself—as if speaking from the greater You. Write down assurances and support. Embrace the power of your greater essence and allow yourself to tune in.

To finish, focus on this feeling of universal energy and tune into how it overlaps your own conscious personality. Write a brief note acknowledging this; even if it's as short and simple as, "I know there's a larger portion of my identity that will always be there for me, which allows me to float on my sea of trust."

FOUR

MARBLES OF WISDOM

A tornado of thought is unleashed after each new insight. This in turn results in an earthquake of assumptions. These are natural disasters that re-shape the spirit.

VERA NAZARIAN, *THE PERPETUAL CALENDAR OF INSPIRATION*

In this chapter, let's choose to focus on two qualities. Both require simply paying attention within the moment.

Ram Dass summed it up beautifully, many years ago: *Be here now.*

The first quality is the ability to perceive infinite beauty everywhere our eyes may roam. To recognize the magnificence in all things: dew drops sparkling in the morning sun; the splendor of a bluebird hopping about with a quizzical eye; the magic of rain splattering against the windowpane.

Another quality to nurture is the ever-present desire to perceive wisdom and insight in every aspect of life. Our reality is glittering with effervescent magic. Potent messages exist everywhere for all who are willing to embrace their inner mystic.

What does that mean?

We so often have no choice but to hurry, bustling about in our busy lives. We may feel trapped by officious duties or *that which absolutely must be accomplished.* It can even become a matter of expediency to turn away from the ordinary delights of life—to train ourselves to ignore in adulthood those everyday miracles that entranced us during our youth. As a child, I couldn't wander past a dandelion bursting into seed without wanting to yank it up, make a wish, take a deep breath and blow, scattering those seeds high into the air. While strolling on a sidewalk, if opportunity arose, I would leap up on any available wall, holding out my arms and balancing as if on a tight rope, high above the ground.

Ah, but we're told now that we are adults. If we dare to leap up, others make look askance. If we can't help but sing along when a favorite tune blasts over the store's speakers, someone pushing a cart may avert their eyes or frown. All those hints or even blatant admonishments train us to shut down. This leads to believing that perhaps we *should* ignore the delight inherent in ordinary circumstances. Even worse, we may become predisposed to judge the sights, smells, and sounds of our world based on the approval of others.

A child has permission to clap hands and squeal with glee at the sight of a yellow balloon bobbing on a string. As adults we may feel expected to ignore the commonplace and instead only to heap praise on what others have declared is extraordinary. Yet the graceful beauty of a purple wildflower dancing tenderly in the wind is as exquisite and meaningful as the sublime creations of our favorite artists.

If we're open to it, insights may pop up even within the

silliest bits of inspiration. One example for me from a few years back was with a catchy pop tune called, "Call Me, Maybe." A bit of fluff that rose up the charts, pleasant and fun but not exactly a philosophical treatise. Yet a morsel caught my ear and danced around in my thoughts, with pleasing results. Because sometimes it's just one line—on a page, in a song, within a quick advert, or on the back of a cereal box. One line nudges your brain or resounds within the heart, soothing and inspiring. The "emotional epiphany" leads to an intuitive understanding that sometimes can be articulated and other times simply experienced. Like a feeling-tone, deep within our souls.

Who knows where those delicious, oh-so-meaningful messages will pop up? Unless we keep eyes and ears open, we could miss all those gleaming pearls the universe gleefully tosses about as if plucked from a bag of marbles.

Marbles of Wisdom?

Why not?

That day, driving along and hearing that song, one line grabbed me.

"Before you came into my life, I missed you so much..."

Isn't it tantalizing? The idea of missing a special someone, even before a first meeting, dances in my mind. How many other special souls might there be whose presence I already miss? All because I have yet to stumble into their particular space. Before chance or good fortune or intuitive timing creates a fork on some internal road and allows us at last to meet.

How many other experiences have I yearned to taste before even knowing those delicious tidbits could exist?

Bright and shiny bits of wisdom hover within every precious moment, they are all just waiting to spark a brilliant light within. Moments designed to induce a tantalizing appetite that beckons, coaxing us to ponder, gently consider, and even become dazzled with wonder. Heed the call when you can, dear friend. It's your soul whispering, urging you to dig deeper and stretch beyond all known boundaries. The more we open inner ears to listen, the more we choose to peer around and truly see, the more the universe reveals herself to be a magical book written specifically for each one of us. Each page bursting at the seams and flush with evocative insights. One of the greatest gifts we can ever offer to our selves is simply to choose to consciously awaken and turn those pages ourselves.

SUGGESTED FOCUS:

Throughout the day, take that extra moment to pause and notice.

Does your coffee cup handle curve pleasantly in your grip? Can you detect individual notes of flavor within your coffee or tea?

Savor your meal, noting every aspect. Is there a particular herb that stands out? Is the texture of one dish more pleasing than the other?

When you step outside, take a deep breath. What fragrances can you detect? Is there a hint of moisture in the air or is it noticeably dry? Look around and view your yard and the landscapes of your neighbors. Which tree is tallest? Peer closely at the leaves, counting how many hues of color you can perceive.

How does the shower feel? Does the shampoo have a pleasing aroma? Feel the water cascading down your back and note how your skin reacts to the temperature.

When you start your car, listen for the sounds and consciously, deliberately note your surroundings. The rumble of the motor, the bright chime as the system awakens, the feel of the seat and even the steering wheel you grip can all be sensory delights.

If you pause to exchange thoughts with a coworker or

someone strolls past you on the street, see how many details you can spot. The hue of a shirt or the style of hair, specific earrings or a colorful tattoo—what stands out?

Note whatever thoughts randomly surface every time you sharpen your focus. Encourage your mind to reflect on possible messages you might be sending yourself.

Let's begin a process of exploration based on awakening within the moment.

When we grip the steering wheel without noticing, or step into the steamy shower; when we distractedly pour a fresh cup of coffee or turn down a familiar street, we often go into autopilot mode. This means we tune out, rather than tuning in. By breaking through the hypnotic lull of familiarity by consciously noticing, we open ourselves up to become more engaged with life which will always be fulfilling and pleasing in itself. Yet we do more. We also nudge open a doorway to our greater awareness. Engaging our senses opens up our mind in ways that are reminiscent of our childhood. This reawakens our desire to speculate, to wonder, and to listen for the wisdom that can arise when we need it most.

AFFIRMATION: <u>*By paying attention in each moment, I open myself up to my own inner wisdom.*</u>

REVIEW:

Jot down what you noticed during this exercise. Pay special attention to any feelings that arose whenever you reminded yourself to tune in. Did your perception of time change when you paused to note details, speeding up or slowing down? Did you find any change in your sensory awareness when you paused to pay attention?

Pick one particular moment point during your attention-exercise. Pretend that this was simply a vivid dream that you can recall. Note how your feelings expand as you explore your memory from this view.

Finally, imagine now the 'dream scene' was a message to you from your greater self. Playfully explore the scene and imagine what message you might be sending to yourself.

FIVE
THE UNIVERSE WHISPERS, "REMEMBER"

As your faith is strengthened you will find that there is no longer the need to have a sense of control, that things will flow as they will, and that you will flow with them, to your great delight and benefit.

EMMANUEL

This morning as I leisurely strolled into my sunny kitchen to brew a cup of English breakfast tea, there he sat, perched precariously on the porcelain wall of my sink. An arachnid—a house spider that, in my view, needed to become an out-of-the-house spider. Clearly, the sink was not a safe place for tiny creatures to linger. I snatched up a water glass and available post card. As I cautiously approached, the little thing dramatically leapt downward, curling up into a ball. The defensive pose touched a chord within me.

Ever so carefully I settled the glass over him, gently scooting the postcard close and waited. I hesitated to shove the card forward—those tiny legs are fragile, so patience was necessary. Bent over, I gazed downward, focusing on surrounding my fellow being with radiant love. The spider remained stock-still, curled up in a protective ball.

How many times have my own trembling fears overwhelmed me in a similar manner? How often have I metaphorically curled up in a ball, anticipating horrid disaster when a benevolent universe wanted nothing more than to protect me?

Often I return to a before-sleep ritual I began to explore a few years back. As I lay snugly cushioned in my comfortable bed, my focus is to surround myself with compassionate, healing, all-accepting love.

Next, I envision gorgeous, loving energy swirling outward, first to encircle my beloved husband, and onward to all those I cherish. The energy continues to radiate with golden tenderness, surrounding my bedroom, then my house, then my block, my neighborhood, state, country, our precious earth, gradually extending out to encompass the entire universe, all surrounded with a brilliant, comforting circle of love.

It brings me peace of heart.

Yet what I know now without a doubt is we also have to choose, quite deliberately, to walk away from the trembling fear. Trusting when we return, we can confidently initiate decisive action and make whatever changes are most beneficial.

After a bit, I revisited the tiny creature who had at last unfurled from his protective stance and was darting nervously under the glass. I whispered gentle assurances as I finished placing the postcard securely against the rim. At last I could cautiously transport him outside. I bent down, tipped the glass onto the dewy lawn. Just like that his reality changed for the better.

The potential threat of faucets splashing water, forcing to him to swirl haphazardly down the drain had vanished. He was safe now, whether or not he was ever aware of the specific potential danger. I felt in that moment like a helper sent by the universe to assist another living being.

A vivid memory arises of another opportunity, back when I was twenty.

At the time, I was living in a small funky-cool suburb near Portland, Oregon. A small town with a large personality, Sellwood was lined with feathery trees amid cozy streets, dotted with eclectic antique stores. My job back then still stands out as a favorite: working as a preschool teacher in an informal setting where children and I would dare to explore creativity and enjoy spontaneous escapades together. Once I suggested we sketch favorite animals on chalkboards, an activity the kids threw themselves into with exuberance. Even better, we then acted out our favorites in a noisy, free spirited environment stuffed full of adventurous experimentation.

They took their cue from me, the only adult in the room. When Timmy asked me to draw an elephant, I couldn't be held back by worries that *I'm no artist.* Gamely, I grabbed the chalk and traced an outline with a vague resemblance to the creature requested. The kids howled, delighted with my fumbling attempts. When I got down on my knees, turning my arm into a makeshift trunk, they scrambled to join me. Imagining how elephants and other wild creatures moved and communicated stretched open our minds. Even better, it was fun for us all. It was a gift to play freely, tuning into their world, uninhibited by the shackles of convention and maturity.

Feeling high on life, as I often did after my day of play-work, I drove home down a small quiet lane. Humming along with the radio, I glanced over to my right just in time to note an elderly woman wearing a black dress and clutching a satin purse as she tottered down the street. In the next instant, I watched, horrified, as she collapsed on the sidewalk. Wrenching the wheel to the right, I pulled up to the curb and leapt out, running over. I knelt to find her dazed and disoriented. She had skinned her elbow and a bit of blood trickled down. She insisted she was fine and back then without cellphones and instant communication, I didn't know what to do. Already she was tugging on my arm and insisting on standing, yet I rebelled against the idea of simply moving on. With gentle persuasion, I managed to convince her to let me drive her home. Once there, I coaxed out the phone number for her daughter and made the call. I perched on her antique sofa in her spotless house, holding her hand as she thanked me repeatedly for driving her home, exclaiming how nice it is to be cared for. My throat tightened while tears tugged at my eyes. How grateful I was to have been driving at the exact perfect moment to help this beautiful soul in a time of need. I felt as if I'd been given a gift, to provide assistance like that.

She crumpled at the exact moment I'd glanced her way.

What if it had been my mom? Or in some far distant future, an elderly me who needed the kindness of a random stranger?

Soon her daughter arrived, bursting in with a flurry of worry and concern. She too thanked me for watching out for her mother. I brushed aside the thanks, murmuring that I was happy to be there at the right time.

A safe universe watches out for us.

Sometimes the universe chooses us to be the helper. There will be a hint of guidance that could pass right by, unless we pay attention.

It's up to us to listen.

An inner voice murmurs to turn left instead of right, to choose to stroll down a particular lane or glance over at pedestrians wandering down the sidewalk. Suddenly we may feel an urge to pause for just a few precious moments before leaving our home. *Bring this, leave that.* Sometimes clues appear so mundane we grow accustomed to ignoring the whispers.

We forget we need to choose to listen.

If only we could forget to fear instead.

Let's spend more time listening to our inner selves. There are delightful tales to hear, delicious encouragement bolstering our souls, brilliant potential insights knocking patiently at inner doors.

It's time to forget to be afraid, just like when we were kids. When we dared to exist with audacious courage and outrageous exuberance. You and I hold more power than we realize. There are lonely moments when we wonder if our life has purpose, if we could possibly make a difference, if only we dare.

Our souls wait patiently for us to remember our connection, to remember that the universe isn't *out there*. It's right here, within you and within me. Yet to remember this is to take a chance on faith, to set aside the fears that keep us ensnared.

We can choose to remember. When we do, the universe encourages us to live heroically, to be the person who cares enough to save a tiny spider. To be the everyday hero who may, by chance and by choice, be a helper to a random stranger on the street.

SUGGESTED FOCUS:

Envision yourself surrounded by love. You may see this as a glowing color—pink, gold, green, blue, whatever hue feels right to you. Surround yourself with this vision of love swirling around you with gentle support. Extend this energy to circle the room you occupy, extending outward to surround your home, your block, your town, your state, your country, until you encircle the world with love. You can also focus on specific people, both those you adore and those with whom you seek healing. Do this exercise for at least one week, though it is a focus that can become a lifelong practice.

Ask the universe for extra support in remembering to love.

As you drift off to sleep, ask yourself to tune into this circle of love. If there are relationships that are troubling, request dreams of healing. You may also ask the universe to give you opportunities to help or heal within your dreams.

AFFIRMATION: A loving universe supports and protects me. I am a vital part of this loving universe. I am guided by love.

REVIEW:

In your notebook, share what feelings arose when you did this nightly exercise. Note if there were changes in the quality of your sleep. Particularly note any dreams that occur following your focus.

*Write down areas of life or relationships that might need extra healing. As you go through your list, consciously utilize your circle of love surrounding you with comfort and protection. You should note a distinct point where you can **feel** increased strength and security as you surround the situation or relationship with loving focus. Hold your focus for five minutes, then write down any thoughts, feelings, or images that arise as a result.*

SIX
TO EXPECT OR NOT EXPECT, THAT IS THE QUESTION

If you never expect the sun to shine, it won't rain any less. But if you expect it sometimes, you gift yourself the happiness of those light rays before they even arrive, and honestly life is truly far too fragile and short for us not to allow happiness to thrive in every opportunity.

CORINDA LUBIN-KATZ

For most of us, expectations play a substantial role in life. Sometimes my own are fulfilled beyond my wildest fantasies. Other times, not so much. Yet these days I rarely feel let down or overly disappointed.

Why?

The reason is simple: my greatest expectation is based on an internal focus, rather than outer results.

I *expect* to learn from every circumstance and *expect* to be responsible for my own satisfaction within every moment. This applies to every anticipated or unexpected situation in life. This knowledge has been a lifesaver.

Expectations can be overwhelming.

At age eight, I auditioned to play a role in a local production of The Sound of Music. Just stepping into that musty theater excited me. The sharp tangy scent of freshly painted backdrops and a sense of hushed anticipation permeated the space.

The week before, a neighboring family generously invited me along as they attended a performance of The Prince and the Pauper. The performance had dazzled my senses and now the idea of actually being on that stage thrilled me beyond comprehension.

My expectations soared when the director told me that I read well. Then came a test I couldn't have anticipated. The same director lined up the hopefuls auditioning according to height. As it turned out, I was too tall to play the youngest character, too short to be the next one up. My fantasy was crushed for a reason that made no sense to me.

The impact of pinning our hopes and dreams on outer circumstances, only to have said hopes smashed against the reality of disappointment, is devastating.

Love 'em or hate 'em, expectations are a part of life.

One guy I knew briefly wanted quite passionately to believe he was the exception to the rule. An online friend with whom I enjoyed conversing, Tom was smart and quick-witted. He often added positive, thoughtful comments on my posts and appeared to share a similar love of philosophy.

At one point, he shared that he held no expectations in life. At all.

"Expectations are the root of all heartache," he announced confidently. A good quote from Shakespeare, I do believe. Yet aren't expectations along the same lines as desire or beliefs? I can't help but quietly chuckle when someone proclaims their fervent desire to hold no desires. Admittedly, many a philosophy insists one should discard desire (rather like the much maligned ego, treated like a bastard child by certain spiritual paths), which doesn't strike me as realistic.

And the last word is pertinent for me.

Realistic.

Expectations should be realistic enough to allow for the foibles of humans and nature. While also being substantial enough to beckon like the tantalizing aroma of fresh-baked chocolate chip cookies.

When I stumble over expectations, it's usually because of a lack of communication. Sometimes the reason is simple, and rather heartbreaking. I believe I "should" live my life in a way that is based on the wants or needs of others. Occasionally, this has been projected onto me. More often than not, I project the dastardly expectation onto myself.

In many ways, childhood is our first training ground, we absorb the unspoken messages without realizing how a frown, a raised eyebrow, or a disapproving glance informs us how we're not living up to some code of conduct that has never been properly spelled out. We also are told in no uncertain terms when we are misbehaving or not living up to expectations in the classroom, in our family home, and in social situations. For those with low self-esteem or who were raised in circumstances where adults were brutally harsh or simply used passive-aggressive techniques rather than spelling out expectations, we can develop a rather extreme habit of just assuming we are always at fault. When this happens, we no longer need any outside source to scold us for falling short for we become our own worst critic.

It can be something as meaningless as *I knew I should have ordered the shrimp fajitas, this cheese enchilada is so unappealing. What an idiot I am for not ordering what I wanted.*

My expectations for myself in that example are straightforward. I *should* know what I want. I *should* order what sounds good. Yet I'm tripping over what could be an easy decision because my fear is that the food won't live up to my expectation. What if the shrimp fajita isn't tasty? Or it's too messy? Whatever, Chiron! It's a minor decision, not a matter of life or death.

Yet for me, it's rooted in a fear of making the wrong move. In my unsupervised childhood where there were very few family dinners, I fended for myself all too often. My elder siblings didn't care if I was fed or not, and my mother apparently assumed I could raise myself. It didn't scar me to subsist on cold sandwiches or bowls of cereal, but it did mean that on those few occasions when we went out to eat, my desire for a cooked meal was overwhelming. This was my chance to choose and eat *whatever I wanted*. The decision was made even more vital because I also had to choose between familiar and favorite dishes that I *knew* would be delicious or take a chance on something unknown. What if it was awful? What if I hated it? There would be no recourse then. I would be stuck with whatever food I'd selected. For a kid subsisting on the blandest of choices over and over in a lonely home, this decision took on greater importance than seems realistic. Yet I can't deny the memory of that fear that seized me whenever I faced the potential dilemma of making the wrong decision. I'll confess that to this day there's still a great reluctance to experiment with foods, though I now am more willing to take a chance.

This fear of choosing incorrectly filtered through my entire life. Whether it was a fear of blurting out the wrong thing or making a poor choice, I often invested countless hours reviewing my decisions.

This is called second-guessing, when being evasive. When blunt, I am forced to recognize it's a way to beat myself up. To scold, or chide, or just slap myself around because I'm not living up to a standard not only unrealistic, but truly pointless. I'll admit my challenging background occasionally arises, a faint shadow of the past. Forgotten memories may still exist to twist me this way and that. Lead me to perhaps occasionally slip into old patterns of self-condemnation or compare myself to a lofty ideal. In reality, those patterns no longer have to be a factor. Here's why: the only moment I will ever personally experience is now.

Both for you and for me, only one moment exists. The one we're experiencing now, as we gently breathe in and confidently breathe out.

Those self-defeating patterns may push me to forget the current moment, to tumble down a rabbit-hole of past patterns.

The solution is clear. It may not be comfortable, but it is beautifully obvious.

Self-acceptance.

As the saying goes, "Warts and all."

Which leads me back to my exploration.

Expectations.

Acceptable or not?

Something to be utilized or just feverishly shoved into the dark corners of my soul?

I vote for acceptable.

You see—I adore having expectations. For example, if you're invited into my home for a steaming cup of English breakfast tea or a glass of rich cabernet, I absolutely expect you *not* to pee on my floor. Does this seem like an absurd and rather extreme argument? Of course! Yet I still remember a time from way back.

My brother had invited me to a party. Wildly insecure at age twenty-one, I'd recently fallen madly in love with a man eight years my senior. Robert M. was intelligent, kind, and nonjudgmental, his love offered me my first glimpse of true acceptance. Though I dressed in thrift store hippie clothes, wore Lennon glasses and no make-up, kept my very long hair tied back in a braid, and felt awkward and out of place, he told me often that I was beautiful, something I just couldn't perceive. Even better, his respect and love made me feel beautiful.

Now, my brother was only a year younger than my boyfriend but nothing like this soft-spoken example of maturity. Jeff enjoyed playing host because it meant he was in charge. His brash, crude, and sexist behavior made me cringe but he was the only father figure I had ever known. I yearned for his approval (a lost hope that would never be fulfilled) and even more desperately yearned that those I loved, like Rob, could somehow respect a brother that shamed and terrified me in ways I could never openly admit.

So we attended the party in a beautiful Portland, Oregon home glowing with dark hardwood floors and jade-green walls. What occurred next was uncomfortable, to say the least. My brother liked to surround himself with sycophants who, like him, drank to excess and partied until they dropped. Which one guy did with embarrassing consequences.

His nickname was Party-Hardy Harvey or something like that. A giant bear of a guy who could laugh uproariously and was always willing to man the keg. After chugging too many beers, he laid down on the floor and just passed out. Rob and I sat on the couch, trying to hang in there, and me, over-compensating as I often did, struggled to be unconditionally nonjudgmental. It worked up until the moment that I saw a dark puddle creeping towards our feet. The source? Party-Hardy Harvey, of course.

I still remember my embarrassed horror as I raised my feet to avoid stepping in the puddle of urine. I snuck a look around to see how others handled it. This guy was their close friend, yet they did nothing but look away. My brother stepped over him, laughing, as if Harvey was simply a pile of dirty laundry to be ignored. I flushed with pity for the guy but was too overwhelmed to even think. I glanced over at my boyfriend. Neither Rob nor I had any words; we just scooted over to avoid soiling our shoes and quietly left.

Returning to my online friend, Tom, what I figured out is that his issue with expectations was his way of making sense out of a situation that hurt him and even better, it offered a solution. He'd hinted about his divorce, how his wife had initiated it and that she'd felt let down due to expectations, which so often is *the word that shall not be named*. He hadn't lived up to her expectations. After their divorce, he'd fallen in love with a woman who would then eventually let him down in turn, and based on what he shared with me, the warning signs were already there. To him it seemed that the problem was not that he'd made mistakes in the past, or that his current girlfriend was taking advantage of his good nature and turning him into her own personal caretaker, the problem was expectations. If there were no expectations, then no one could crush them.

Always a heartbreaking fear.

My friend eventually did break up with his girlfriend and as sometimes happens with online friendships, we drifted apart. I'd see his posts pass by occasionally and was happy to see he'd found another girlfriend and appeared to be genuinely happy.

I expected no less.

Everyone has expectations, whether we admit them or not.

Which means, yes, boundaries (and the knowledge of them) are useful. My desire and my expectation is to have friends who take pleasure in being kind—who are playful in spirit and open-minded. Friends with the ability to reason and explore ideas, and who also strive for compassion, tolerance, and self-awareness.

I'm expecting they seek the same, which is why they're likewise drawn to me.

Another bonus point for this much-maligned word is in

relation to our journeys in life. My desire to live up to my own expectations motivates me to dig deeper. I'm motivated to investigate intriguing topics, to enthusiastically adventure, and challenge myself in dozens of ways. Perhaps my acquaintance's point in avoiding expectations was based on a fear of those previously mentioned high standards. However, the idea of perfection should be stricken from any and all lists. Excellence is a goal I hope to occasionally meet, but perfection feels way too confining (not to mention unrealistic). Perfection implies a static state, a definitive ending point. Yet change is the only constant, and throughout our lives we are continuously evolving—exploring, discovering, and becoming our selves.

Which is why recognizing the idea of choice is vital. If we develop a healthy and realistic attitude towards expectations, we can choose friends and lovers who share a similar perspective. What value could I possibly gain from jumping through hoops of unrealistic goals?

For me, a yearning for friends who strive, as I do, for a focus of self-awareness makes it easier to form lasting bonds. Anyone with a small measure of accountability under their belt knows we all have daunting challenges to meet, trembling fears to conquer. I'll choose folks who recognize this.

I'll seek out those consciously stepping away from the debilitating roles of being an enabler/rescuer/caretaker, along with those folks who recognize the seductive futility of feeling put upon by the outside world. If I choose well, then they will have no pressing need to project unrealistic expectations on me, and visa versa. They will expect courtesy and respect, kindness and reciprocity. They'll look for a measure of decency in my soul, and a willingness to examine my behavior and be the best person I can be in any given moment.

Which really is no more than I ask of myself.

To be honest about, and with, our selves is quite an achievement, after all.

My friends are not expecting perfection.

The world does not require my perfection.

Which makes it safe to say:

"I'm not perfect."

Deep breath.

Again: "I'm not perfect."

Isn't that a liberating statement?

Even better:

"I don't have to be perfect to be loved and accepted."

This is the secret charm of the movie, *Bridget Jones' Diary*, after all. Don't we all want to be loved *just the way we are?*

Message from the universe:

"You are loved, just the way you are."

Sure, there will be some expectations, generated by you, and by others. Yet the genuine, heart-felt purpose of expectation is not to intimidate or control but to motivate us all to be the best we can be within every moment.

We are sun-tipped daisies reaching for the bluest of skies. Those fluttering petals don't have to be perfect, and the puffy clouds offer graceful contrast and occasionally nourishing rain. The fresh breezes can clear our hearts, sweep away any lingering fears, and when at last the gentle night eases in, we can rest easy. Anticipating a restful sleep, we can stretch luxuriously in our bed without fear. Expecting a shower to invigorate us or a meal to bring us satisfaction is not unrealistic; it's how we go about our days.

It's useful, productive, and healing to set aside unrealistic expectations, especially those that demand perfection (of ourselves or others) or those that are based on fear. Yet even now I'm chuckling remembering an old commercial that utilized Carly Simon's song, "Anticipation" to suggest that the slow-moving ketchup was worth the wait. Because yes, anticipation can be as tasty as the meal itself. We give up too much when we sacrifice expectations on an altar built out of worry and dread. Instead, let's utilize them not with a panicky religious fervor but with an artistic perspective. We can recognize how they inform us to our beliefs. Even better we can alter them to serve us and help us to anticipate the best life has to offer.

SUGGESTED FOCUS:

Examine personal expectations about your friends, family, work, and internal goals with a short list beginning with the words, I Expect. *Decide which expectations are realistic, productive, and satisfying. Consider how to modify those that do not fit this criteria.*

"I expect outer circumstances to bring me happiness" can be changed to "I expect to find purpose and insight, which will bring me joy or satisfaction in every circumstance."

Take extra time with those expectations that are painful or scary. Expectations like, "I expect others will think I'm too loud," "I expect I'll make a fool out of myself," are indications of distorted beliefs that need to be addressed carefully. Those expectations are based on conditioning and are now part of a running program in your mind that, whether you consciously realize it or not, are influencing how you interact with others and how you participate in life.

Your expectations can draw to you circumstances that will align with those hidden beliefs. If you're expecting others will think poorly of you—will think you're too loud or too quiet or too something—you may unwittingly ignore every person who doesn't match that hidden belief. To put it simply, if you're expecting frowns, you may unconsciously turn away from the smiles because it doesn't match your expectation.

"I expect those who enjoy me for who I am will notice and appreciate me, and I am worthy of notice and appreciation," can be a healthy reframe.

Rather than ignoring or suppressing expectations, it's vital to open up to examining them with a clear eye. Aim to spend at least seven days with this focus, writing down expectations and exploring what beliefs are revealed. As you reframe any expectations, recognize the power and potency of your choice. Write your modified expectations on a separate page for study.

AFFIRMATION: *I am comfortable examining my expectations and recognize that I am in charge of my expectations. Knowing this, I expect to perceive the best in life and the best within myself.*

REVIEW:

Utilizing your notes of initial expectations and your list of modified expectations, jot down how these new expectations feel to you. What emotions arise? There may be memories that surface and it can be useful to note where and how these expectations were first formed or accepted.

Consider writing out some alternate scenarios, even a paragraph is useful, where you explore how a situation might have turned out if you hadn't adopted that expectation. What choices might you have made with your new, modified expectation? You can also spend time simply considering this in a meditative state, consciously day-dreaming about alternative events.

Incorporate a daily habit of noting when expectations arise and examining whether they are productive, healthy, and pleasing. If they don't serve you in a positive way, deliberately change them on the spot.

SEVEN
NO IS A COMPLETE SENTENCE

Courage is the most important of all the virtues because without courage, you can't practice any other virtue consistently.

MAYA ANGELOU

From my earliest years, establishing boundaries was a fearsome challenge.

Like many a child raised in abusive or chaotic situations, I learned to adapt. As abuse survivors, we bury feelings, bite our tongues, reluctantly accept a reality that years later we realize made no sense.

In oppressive environments, saying no is often not permitted. Objections of any kind are forbidden. This type of background can painfully scar the psyche. Relinquishing patterns carved into our minds in our youngest years takes immense courage and strength. Those unconsciously adopted patterns make us feel unsafe even as an adult. Until we let them go, we may feel intimidated by others without even knowing why.

When I was about nineteen, I remember meeting this guy who would eventually become the boyfriend of someone I knew. When I met him, Peter seemed nice enough but I was distinctly uneasy around him. He reminded me of my brother, which as it turns out, is a comparison he'd find repugnant as he had little respect for my eldest sibling. Yet the connection was there because there was a vague resemblance and even though they were nothing alike, the scars on my psyche burned painfully. It would be many years before I could examine this and recognize the response was not logical but emotional and fear-based.

Part of the programming that we incorporate is focused on our ideas of accountability. When we embrace accountability (whether because others insist we're at fault or we choose to own the authority of our choices) we may find ourselves taking on too much responsibility—leading up to becoming a scapegoat for those who have taken the opposite path.

There is a tendency to be on one side of blame or the other. We take responsibility or we don't.

Some adapt to an oppressive environment through absolute submission. If my rage-filled stepfather shouted that somebody better clean the goddamned floor, you can bet I crashed to my knees quickly and began frantically scrubbing.

Others fight back with screams of defiance or find smaller victims on whom they can unleash their pent-up fear-induced anger. For several years, beginning at age eight, I endured being forced to the ground, pinned in place while my fourteen-year-old brother screamed into my face. He tormented me mercilessly until I howled, tears flowing as I begged for release. Spending a summer with my grandmother on the opposite coast, blissfully free from the terror of abuse, I often shrieked myself awake as I struggled with horrific nightmares of being chased and held down.

In later years, my studies in psychology helped me to understand. He too was shattered by horrific events beyond his control; his broken soul found no solace. Our stepfather tormented him as well. I have vivid memories of Ray chasing him with a wire hanger, beating him and yelling, "Big boys don't cry!"

My sibling's anxiety coupled with the debilitating shame that results from feeling like an unwanted child. This was a shame we all shared. My brother's terror matched my own, yet I suspect it was my quaking fear that angered him the most. He saw within me a reflection of his own dread, and being a teenage boy struggling to find strength and confidence in an abusive home, I was a mirror he wanted to shatter.

I wasn't a target.

I just happened to be in the way.

So we learn through our interpretation of our experiences to believe ourselves to be responsible for everything around us, or completely blame free. We internalize or externalize the accountability.

The two most common slots in which we file ourselves are:

1. *It's not my fault!*

or

2. *It's always my fault.*

My coping mechanism with my abuse was to internalize. To believe that I was responsible for everything that occurred.

It's always my fault.

If only I was better, then people wouldn't hurt me.

He's angry and I must have done something wrong to deserve this.

For those of us who internalize, who take on too much accountability, saying No and establishing boundaries feels almost unethical. As if some unspoken moral code lodged deep within our psyche obligates us to consent. Whether the acquiescence is to go along with requests we'd rather refuse, or to permit ourselves to be locked into abusive situations, it can feel wrong to say, "No."

The rest of my family externalized and began believing the outside world was at fault. It's rather like knocking over a glass and blaming the glass for being in the way. *Stupid glass.*

I remember in later years watching my elderly mom yank too hard on the chain dangling on the pretty lamp I'd picked up for her. Yank, yank, yank, until the lamp no longer functioned. "Stupid lamp," she'd mutter. "It never works properly."

When I was a kid, a landlord managed to peek inside our apartment (Mom always kept the shades firmly drawn) and noting the mess—newspapers scattered about, a lamp perched haphazardly on top of a flimsy overturned box—told her there were standards required to live there. My mom erupted in fury. How dare he look inside the apartment when she answered the door! More like *how dare he judge me for the deplorable living conditions that I damn well know about, which is why the freaking curtains are drawn.*

There was always a reason we had to move, often suddenly and always with haphazard anger fueling the frenzied packing.

It's not my fault!

One incident highlighted my mom's desperation to avoid accountability.

She was hurriedly picking me up from school. Dad had died the year before, and here I was in kindergarten at age four. It was the easiest solution for her problem of feeling forced to parent us, to shove me in school as quickly as possible. Often I'd forget to bring home the sweater I'd worn, but I never remember her actually verifying whether I had it at the end of day. Instead, she'd complain bitterly about how the teacher should be making sure it was on me before I walked out the door. As if a teacher keeping track of twenty kids was shirking her duty, simply because my mom didn't have the patience to walk up with me and grab the sweater herself, or even ask the teacher to make sure I had it before I left.

In retrospect, I understand her frustration, but remembering her oft-vocalized discomfort over feeling stuck in the role of motherhood still stings. I'm grateful that when we reached adulthood, she'd soften and learn how to love. No matter her prickly issues in our childhood, she worked hard to help out the offspring who grew up to be dysfunctional adults.

However those days are far into the future for childhood me, who is patiently waiting outside of Westminster Christian School, my first encounter with formal education.

She pulled up to the curb and jumped out to retrieve me, yanking me towards the green Oldsmobile my dad had purchased the year before he'd died. She was clearly impatient to be off. Often it was so she could make it to the bar to grab a quick drink before picking up my brother and sister. Looking back, I still feel baffled trying to understand her feelings. As a child, this was my life so I rarely questioned, even when Mom told us how we drove her crazy, that we were a bother and a distraction, that we were unwanted—that she wished we had died instead of our father.

At age four I wasn't yet old enough to consciously register her disapproval, and I adored being in school. This was the first time I remember actually having a measure of attention. Even better, I was being taught to read.

Mom seemed distracted, as she nearly always was. Not one to ask how my day was or whether I'd learned anything interesting, she simply opened the door, put me in the front seat and slammed the door shut.

When she got in and started the car I spoke.

I said quietly, "Mommy, my finger's in the door."

Her head whipped around, and she began screaming. Naturally I began screaming too. As she yanked open the door, my finger began to hurt terribly. My shrieks and tears reached a fever pitch.

Mom dragged me up to the school nurse who patiently comforted me as she wrapped my bloody finger in a secure bandage. What occurred next summed up the focus of my family. It required her only to speak four words.

"It's not my fault."

My mom ignored my fear, my shock, my bleeding, throbbing finger, and focused solely on redirecting blame.

I hurt you because of your actions, or because of this outside circumstance.

The belief that I deserved inattention or even pain became an unconscious theme in my life. The seeming random events of a chaotic childhood stitched together a pattern that I then unconsciously used to pick and choose potential friends and lovers.

Our lifelong quest, whether we realize it consciously or not, is to become self-aware. We'll pull towards us people and events to trigger awareness. As Carl Jung stated, "Until you make the unconscious conscious, it will direct your life and you will call it fate."

Microcosm to macrocosm.

Whether we faintly understand or completely ignore our personal beliefs, those beliefs will force their way towards us, striving to make us aware by echoing back to us from the world at large. Our unconscious fears will attract bullies to intimidate us or larger-than-life antiheroes who appear fearless. Similarly we may pull towards us people who radiate like the dawning sun, folks whom we admire, who reflect qualities we yearn for within our own personalities. People with a gigantic presence may drop into our sphere of consciousness, reflecting back what we are unable to perceive within ourselves.

Those who feel constantly at fault can be drawn to those who evade responsibility for their actions, and visa versa. They fit the imbalanced shadows in our souls.

It seemed that compassion came easier to me than for those in my family and for this I am grateful. Embracing my growing empathy saved me from falling into patterns of casual cruelty. Because of the bad example of others, recognizing the impact of my actions became essential.

<u>It's vital to recognize that if another triggers us, there is a corresponding belief within ourselves.</u> A pattern to be revealed, a button they can push. Otherwise, we'd simply note the situation and move on.

Well, that person certainly is annoying, we may think, *but who cares? That's their problem.* Unless the "problem" is jabbing a finger pointedly at something within us that our unconscious insists we need to perceive.

Yet if people react strongly and we don't feel a corresponding irritation, chances are we're triggering *them*. We can strive to minimize whatever irritation is rubbing painfully against their issues.

We can feel empathy because we also have internal bruises.

Even if we fervently believe we've worked through this or that issue, we drew someone to us to show there's still some healing to be done. Maybe by forgiving this inadvertent shadow that dropped into our life, we can heal a wound from farther back than we consciously remember.

So it's a balancing act, this moving into self-awareness. We can, and should, establish boundaries, firmly and without hesitation. The helpful phrase coined awhile back is the best reminder: *No is a complete sentence.*

"No."

Yet we must recognize and allow for our human frailties. It's vital to acknowledge and perceive how easily those with a compassionate bent can be manipulated with guilt and obligation, with demonstrative tears and dramatic pronouncements. We may be persuaded to think, "How cruel must I be to ignore the wailing and attention-getting theatrics? I really should ignore the nagging inner suspicion this is all a game designed to play me for a fool."

No is a complete sentence.

It's funny but one of the oddest phenomenons is to recognize those most deeply wounded can find it difficult to cry. We learned to keep the prickling tears contained.

It's always my fault.

Often because more dramatic ones loudly insisted revealing our fear or humiliation was too painful for them to bear.

It's not my fault.

So one sibling raged as loudly as my stepfather. The other would simply dodge all responsibility and shift the blame to others. My mother made it clear that revealing any unhappiness, discomfort, or disappointment would be more agonizing than the pain itself, so the lesson instilled was: Keep it to yourself (or *you* are unbearably cruel).

In time, the stereotypes from my earliest years became part of my psychological profile. I'd unconsciously choose friends who echoed the same patterns. I wised up to the most obvious abuse, so learned early on to choose people without a violent temper. Yet as a child I found myself repeatedly drawn to narcissistic friends. Those who could in a heartbeat produce dramatic tears, artfully pleading with others for assurances they were not responsible for the destructive results of their actions. With those friends I remained loyal and complicit, just as I was trained to do with my family.

I kept silent.

The good girl.

If you too have ever experienced the fear that arises when faced with those who insist on your silence, I am here to lend courage and support. I recognize the agony that accompanies the fear. When we are told that assertiveness of any kind is *bad*, and to be *good* means tolerating destructive behavior, it is blatant manipulation.

No is a complete sentence.

Hear me when I say, souls are not born to be bad or good. Those who don't know better may exhibit callous disregard or ruthlessly abuse the trust of others. They may torment or manipulate, use or discard without any recognition of the cruelty of their choices.

Yet we are all struggling to grow and to learn. Perhaps some are still too broken inside to be accountable, to face the stark truth of their actions and beliefs. Our own choices may at times be horribly destructive, and other times so beautifully constructive our heart sings. A fraction of seekers may be far enough along to recognize the ramifications of each choice. Others may be so blind they casually destroy without ever perceiving the horrific consequences of their actions. It takes clarity and compassion to recognize the value of love.

Despite the temptation to rage in turn, to despise those who would exploit our tender hearts, we must remember hatred accomplishes nothing. Hatred simply amplifies and feeds pain, while forgiveness offers clarity, helping us to heal. We forgive because it allows our wounds to heal.

Yet sometimes external circumstances trigger our fear.

What then?

Whether the challenges arise within a frustrating workplace, debilitating early life, or catastrophic political landscape, we choose to move forward. Focus on what we desire to accomplish, rather than dwelling on our fears.

We take charge.

We acknowledge constructive effort is required. We make choices to support goals and take action to move us forward, one step at a time. Speak your truth firmly, recognizing people who trigger our fury or hatred are broken in ways we cannot perceive. Recognize how acting on anger is akin to splashing gasoline onto a raging fire. Striving for constructive choice is like tossing buckets of cool, flame-quenching sand onto the inferno.

If you are struggling with echoes of lingering agony within your personal life, take heart.

We are healing our selves and each other.

Shine your light, if that be your gift. Play your hopeful tunes, write inspiring stories, paint evocative pictures, dig fingers into the fertile earth and plant nutritious food and flowers, gently stretch into yoga positions, let your precious body flow in dance.

If your passion is activism, then write thoughtful essays and pointed letters. Attend marches! Stand up for the rights and needs of others. Choose your fight but stay objective.

Know that every contribution matters.

The world needs those who march; the world needs those who create.

Boundaries matter. Draw your line in the sand freely and help others feel comfortable with their choices too.

We're all in this together! Now and forevermore will our souls echo with hope.

Shine your light!

Help guide our souls home.

Together in love.

SUGGESTED FOCUS:

If saying No is still a troublesome choice, visualize a situa-

tion where you're being challenged in this regard. It may be something as ordinary as being asked for a quick favor, "Can you just do this one thing for me?" It can also be a stressful event already in the works where you feel obligated to participate.

Visualize yourself in this situation and firmly say, "No." Do not explain or justify or offer any further reason.

"No."

In your focus, examine the feelings that arise. Remind yourself that you are not responsible for the feelings of others, only for your own well being. Visualize yourself saying, Yes to *your* choice. When you give yourself permission to say No freely, your Yes will bring you joy.

AFFIRMATION: <u>I respect and honor my boundaries. When I say No to unwanted obligations, I say Yes to myself.</u>

REVIEW:

In your notebook, jot down any memories of when you felt uncomfortable saying No. Visualize the same incident with a completely different ending. Vividly create a scenario in which you are comfortable saying, No. Often this exercise will trigger feelings: fear, shame, guilt, dread, and sometimes even relief. Note the feelings and continue this exercise until you reach a state of comfortable strength.

Did objections arise? If so write them down and examine them carefully. These are hidden beliefs trying to surface.

Here's a sample:

"I really should go along with this because I have the time and there's no excuse." (Except I don't want to!)

"If I was a good person I'd just say yes, what's the big deal?" (Except I don't want to!)

"This person would be there for me if I needed them so I REALLY SHOULD do this." (Except I don't want to!)

Practice this exercise until you feel comfortable and assured with your ability to say no.

Write down: <u>I don't have to explain why I don't want to do that, because No is a complete sentence.</u>

PART TWO

SELF-IMAGE: WHO MIGHT I BE?

EIGHT
THE QUESTION OF ME

This girl in the mirror
gazes into my soul. As a child I'd press
face into glass, trying to peer
beyond the reflection. To see
Her
in the other world where
dreams reside.

Where is me? Who is me?

Sometimes I trip over my tongue,
blurt out thoughts which spill over the
edge, forming puddles which entrance
    but sometimes
stain. Must be careful to not leave
    footprints in shame.

A whisper of faith, a puff of wind
supporting hummingbird wings. A
    blur of
motion, too fast to track. Fears dart in to
    sip, need
sweet trust to ease a scratchy hunger
    to be
free.

Freedom sighted, a rare bird
this ever-evolving identity,
this determined-to-break-through-the
    shell nestling,
cracking open a personality to create
and become
Me.

I tremble, at times with a whisper that
    quakes, dare I speak
up when others look down? Hiding
    behind make-up
tests designed by a hidden hand behind
    the scenes.

Only one voice sings this inner melody.
A meandering tune with kernels of hope
    and volcanic passion,
freckled dreams warbling like a
    nightingale
on a moonlit eve.

Glimpses through a cluttered forest of
planted beliefs, where shadows fall and
    fragrant seedlings struggle
to remember the soul who is me, who
yearns to be.

I wander through flashes of memories
brushing aside sharp branches that
    scrape.
Somewhere deep within, an ancient
awareness offers respite and assurance.
Despite any shadows that linger,
I awaken to discover who Me just might
Be.

Still a child of wonder, with knobby
    knees
and eyes so wide she can glimpse stars
twinkling in a smile.
A fledgling adult whose wings
    impatiently yearn
to stretch,
to soar beyond the familiar sun. Is the
    crescent moon calling?
I am daring to become
Me.

Within lies an eternal soul who
    nods and
whispers encouragement to the
    fragments of a shell I cracked
open,
who giggles and prances
like a forever child dancing to a robin's
    tune
composed
one fluttering heartbeat at a time.

I am
Bravely
Me.

NINE
BRAVELY ME

I will not ask that you approve. The wild thyme is itself nor asks consent of rose nor reed.

MURIEL STRODE, MY LITTLE BOOK OF PRAYER

Bravery is believing in yourself.

These five words reflect a potent truth that rings throughout the ages. The most courageous act we will ever perform is to pin our treasured hopes and most elusive dreams on a self we're just getting to know.

Did I just say *getting to know*?

I did indeed.

It's a tantalizing notion, as it clicks beautifully into place.

We're self-portraits in motion.

We wield the brush, select a colorful palette of appealing character traits, then jump into the messy business of splashing paints onto our canvas of life. We are all within a lifelong process of discovering, exploring, and becoming our selves.

Who am I?

There's the billion-dollar question right there. Who am I? Which of the many selves I portray within my lifetime is actually, truly me?

Is it the me who is a loving wife, or a loyal friend, or a jovial co-worker? Or the me who has scattered memories, hidden fears, delicious yearnings, and lofty goals?

There's also the childhood me who leapt into the air and danced in front of a mirror, pretending her hairbrush was a microphone, singing along with the Supremes. I remember with tender affection the determined me who hesitantly strummed a C chord, struggling to play an old Rolling Stones tune, "You Can't Always Get What You Want." (But if you try sometimes, you get what you need.)

As a child what I truly *needed* was clear: to believe in the budding personality I hesitantly called my self. Just as we all do.

Studying the numerous pop psychology books my mom carted home flung open windows in my mind. I began to perceive myself with a more multidimensional perspective. The idea of how beliefs form our identity broke apart the idea of a fixed personality.

I believe myself to be optimistic, therefore I am.

I believe I am afraid of ridicule, therefore I am.

Accompanying the fascinating examples of psychological patterns were insights from astrology. At first I hung out in brightly lit grocery stores, flipping through astrology magazines, reading about the various components of a natal chart. A skinny, nearsighted fifteen-year old turning those magazine racks into a makeshift library. Bits and pieces of info being filed away for use. I learned to grasp astrology through an artist's perspective, by training myself to perceive the aspects in a chart like colors on a canvas. I could *see* the difference of Moon in Aquarius or Moon in Capricorn by studying the charts of just about everyone I'd encounter.

Later I'd pore through dozens of astrology books striving to master a metaphysical science that fascinated me. It pleases me to recognize I approached my studies as if living in a different time, a time when apprentices studied to be journeymen, and onward to become a master. At age fifteen, I decided it would be at least ten to fifteen years of dedicated study and practice before I could claim mastership.

How could one resist the lure of such a fascinating exploration? Studies that offered insight into the psychology of my own self, and the selves of every soul encountered throughout my life.

I still remember the shock rippling through me when I first read about Saturn's influence in the chart. The statement: Saturn conjunct the Sun, or Saturn in the first house of your chart can signify a father figure who is absent or tyrannical.

Saturn is conjunct my Sun and also in my first house.

My father died when I was three years old. Definitely absent.

When I was eight, Mom met the man who would be the only other significant relationship in her life. Ray fit the bill of a tyrannical father figure to the letter. Double whammy.

Weird.

That hooked me. The more information I uncovered while studying my natal chart, and the charts of friends and family, the weirder it got. I had no idea *why* it worked. Yet as I discovered how to perceive the various elements of a chart within myself, and in the charts of many others, the more I realized every person is a complex formula of circumstance and aspects of personality.

This also provided a sense of security I'd not known before.

Seeing my personality spelled out so accurately allowed me the luxury of perceiving myself from the outside looking in. Objectivity versus subjectivity. This one shift gave me a sense of strength never before known. Even better, the insights into the personalities of others offered a perspective that elicited compassion and an edge in understanding what makes people tick.

Psychology and astrology opened the rabbit hole of self-awareness. I jumped in with equal measures of glee and relief.

In my late teens, I picked up a used paperback by Hermann Hesse. *Demian* shared the story of Sinclair Lewis. The hero, a young boy who struggled to make sense of the dichotomy between his urges to be one with the light, and the dark fear of actually being draped in shadows. I identified with this conflicted hero whose exploration echoed my own misgivings within a world that could appear rigidly ensconced in extremes. Religion as portrayed in the Old Testament painted a gruesome picture where holy men were ordered to prove their loyalty by killing an only son, and women who questioned were temptresses or blamed for the downfall of humankind. Even worse, the idea that insisted every soul is a sinner for no other reason than they exist. The urge to reason, to question, to seek greater truths, even to dare to know those truths were seen as heroic in a young Jesus, yet a sign of impudent arrogance in a mortal girl.

Who am I?

Was I a child of light?

The love that suffused me at times nearly choked me with tears. I strove to do good deeds, not because a religion or authority figure instructed me to do so. The reason was simply because it felt good, It felt *right* to be kind, to be helpful, to be of service to the world.

Yet like many, I cowered from my darkness, fearful of the

rage that exploded through me when confronted with the violence of others.

While sorting through the clutter of my mom's house after her death, I cracked open a musty box. Inside were the scattered remains of my childhood toys. One toy really stood out. The memories that arose were suffocating.

I picked up a doll from long ago that resembled my eldest cousin, Judy. The doll was part of a set popular in the sixties. *The Littlechap Family* was slightly larger than Barbie dolls in size and represented an idealized Kennedy-like family with a set of four: Dr. John, his wife Lisa, and the two daughters named Judy and Libby. They were given to me when I was four or five.

A year after my father's death, we were finally back home with my mom. As she often worked nights, she chose my cousin to babysit us. Judy was only a couple of years older than my brother and just as volatile. I remember one episode when she was screaming at us that *No, we couldn't have any food after supper.* Defying her unreasonable authority, Jeff opened the fridge to grab a snack. She took ahold of that door and tried to crush his head inside.

It was during one of those terror-filled nights that I disappeared. When Mom came home, my bed was empty. I was discovered, hours later, frantically pedaling my trike alongside Pacific Coast Highway. Trying to escape. The story was that I was sleepwalking or sleep biking, as the case may be, and it was dismissed as if it were an adorable adventure. *Imagine! A little girl like that, out after midnight taking her trike for a spin.*

The fact that PCH was a busy highway with cars and trucks zipping by at manic speed, and I was clearly trying to escape... something...was brushed aside. I managed to make it over a mile away before they found me.

When I picked up the doll, memories rushed in. How could I have forgotten? The doll's brown hair had been haphazardly chopped off, making her more closely resemble my feared and hated cousin. That was not what stood out.

The plastic body had been stabbed.

Round puncture marks, probably from a pencil, dotted the torso. This proof of my own fearful violence shook me. I vaguely remembered my rage as I stabbed at that makeshift voodoo doll, symbolically killing off one of the many monsters that refused to stay safely under the bed.

Was I a child of darkness?

Carl Jung, who suggested that people are fragmented early and may spend a lifetime putting the pieces together, explored shadows through a different lens. He revealed an idea that clicked with me: to be an integrated individual requires one to recognize that all aspects of being—the light and the shadows—must be accepted in order to be whole. Otherwise, we fear those shadowy aspects, disown parts of our own personality, which leaves us lopsided and sometimes even broken.

I briefly touched on the concept of shadow integration in Chapter Six.

Let's dive in a little deeper.

In the classic story of Dr. Jekyll and Mr. Hyde, the lead character develops a split personality based on a potion Jekyll creates. When he downs the noxious fluid he undergoes a complete transformation, both in physical appearance and personality, changing from the refined and gentle Dr. Jekyll into the ferocious Mr. Hyde.

The concept of a split psyche is demonstrated with the doctor being kind, polite, yet not necessarily assertive, and Hyde representing the hidden or disowned aspects of personality. Hyde then becomes a monster with no boundaries that acts out in every situation where the good doctor might feel repressed. Dr. Jekyll yearns for a woman yet is too shy to confess his desire. Hyde feels no such hesitation: he takes what he wants. If someone is rude to Jekyll, the doctor bites his tongue, his alter-ego instead cruelly beats the man down.

It's been portrayed as a metaphor for alcoholism, an idea that works because often alcohol does create a doorway for people to release their repressed shadows—the hidden monster—during a blackout.

Yet the story is even more significant when viewed purely through a psychological lens. In this case, imagine that a person who is fearful of his aggression instead encounters others who represent this 'hidden monster.' In some cases, this means we draw to us people who are overly aggressive, brutish and pushy, which then serves to prove to us what we secretly fear to be true: assertiveness is *bad*. We seek out versions of Mr. Hyde to prove to ourselves that this *shadow* is indeed monstrous.

It's not always so clear cut, though. Were it as shockingly revealing as Dr. Jekyll's alter ego, we might catch on much more quickly. Instead we may find ourselves overreacting to minor assertiveness, feeling irrationally irritated by *that one coworker* who speaks up when we don't. For reasons beyond our conscious grasp, we may also attract people who push us around or bully us. *Why do they single me out?* We scratch our heads baffled. If we're striving to always be nice and reasonable, why do we seem to constantly encounter people who give us such grief?

These encounters are quite beautifully displaying the shadow aspect that we are fearfully hiding from our conscious understanding. A pertinent example is how many people with homophobic issues often lash out because of a denial of their own sexuality. They hate what they fear the most.

Sometimes the shadow aspects aren't hated but they are still disowned. We may think we could never be strong like the hero we fervently admire—the brash one who confronts others without even a speck of hesitation. We may ignore their faults, make excuses for their behavior, because they represent a quality we unconsciously feel is missing in our own personality. Whether we unreasonably idealize or abhor any person, we're grappling with an unacknowledged aspect of our own being.

In my last essay, I confided that one of the shadow aspects of my childhood dealt with my own fear of assertiveness. My response was textbook in that I unreasonably admired those like my sister who took what they wanted, without conscience or regret. Years later, I would recognize the difference between courageous and reckless, but as an anxious, often terrified child, that capacity for self-understanding had yet to be developed.

A big turning point for me was at fifteen when I first read the book, *Psycho-Cybernetics*, by Maxwell Maltz, a plastic surgeon. This international bestseller was the result of his research into how our subconscious self-image creates the idea of who we are, how that impacts our life, and how we can successfully reprogram our self-image to achieve happiness.

Dr. Maltz had a highly successful practice, so successful that he published the book, *New Faces, New Futures: Rebuilding Character with Plastic Surgery*, twenty years before, detailing case histories where plastic surgery, most notably correcting facial flaws, had changed the lives of many patients. These changes in physical appearance also resulted with quite a few quickly and dramatically altering their personality and finding apparent happiness as a result.

Twenty years later though one thing truly nagged at him. Some of his patients showed no change in personality, nor did they react as most had—with a quick (within three weeks) and obvious elevation of self-esteem and self-confidence. Instead, they remained locked in feelings of inadequacy and inferiority. He realized that there was another factor, a "face of personality" that had nothing to do with outer appearance and everything to do with self-image. Yet if not based on outer appearance, what was the mysterious source of our self-image?

He dug deeper still to grasp the psychology of personality, how self-image defines what we think we can do or not do, what we can be or not be. Why some people are "Success-type personalities," or "Happiness prone." Self-image psychology was explored along with the idea of cybernetics, which is the goal-striving, goal-oriented behavior of mechanical systems. We program ourselves, like we program our computer. Our beliefs are what we put in, our self-image is what comes out.

Self-image begins with our beliefs. Beliefs about who we are and what people perceive when they gaze in our direction.

That's how our story begins and how it is constantly reinforced.

My stories were straightforward, or so I believed.

One story, based on my mother's early feedback, stated clearly that I was unwanted and unlovable. The theme played out for years, with me believing I should be grateful for any scrap of attention. This also plagued me with anxiety and general fearfulness. Oddly enough, when we buy into a belief like that, we must reject any proof that goes to the contrary.

It was a chilly day in the San Bernardino Mountains when I clambered onto the school bus on my way to third grade. We'd just recently landed in Crestline, California, having already frantically moved several times since Dad died. Yet another new classroom where I would feel alienated. The third school for me and once again, feeling like the freakish outsider.

As soon as the bus driver wrenched open the double-doors, I darted up the steps, claimed a seat, and scooted over close to the window. Window seats always felt safer, less exposed. I could minimize my presence. My breath fogged up the glass letting me draw little faces or hearts. Shortly afterwards, a schoolmate ambled down the aisle. He was one of the cutest boys in class, dark curly hair, gorgeous blue eyes. Many of my classmates harbored a secret crush. He paused and then plopped down next to me.

There's no way to normalize my response.

I quickly swiveled, put my feet on the long seat and kicked him right off.

Mouths agape, the whole busload of kids turned to watch in horrified fascination.

Undeterred, my classmate, Scott, picked himself up off the dusty floor and sat back down. Appalled, I kicked him off again.

And again.

And again.

Finally, my anger rose to a fever pitch, I shakily stormed up the aisle of that moving bus to complain.

That...boy...keeps trying to sit next to me!

The bus driver glanced my way. Even now I remember his bemused expression. How to handle this? Finally he said gently, "Maybe he likes you."

The emotional response triggered within shook me so violently, my whole body trembled with rage. That was just crazy, insane, unbelievable. Like *me?*

A monster like me?

"No," I spit out. "That can't be it."

I stomped back to my seat, trembling with anger, pointedly ignoring the boy who dared to like me.

My response was actually quite reasonable in that I was staying true to my story of being an unlovable child. The real issue was that I was owning a destructive story rather than rewriting it. Years later, my first boyfriend reflected my own distorted self-image and treated me dismissively and finally with humiliating cruelty. He gave to me what I unconsciously believed that I deserved.

The realization that self-image is responsible for how we see ourselves, regardless of physical appearance—such as *I must be unlovable because I am unloved*—allows us to perceive the potent power of our beliefs. My lifelong quest to understand just who it is that I might be, galvanized me. As the decades flashed by, I devoured hundreds of books seeking understanding.

A straightforward message filtered through, repeated in many guises.

Discover your self.
Create your self.
Own your self.
Know your self.
Be your self.

As I matured I recognized a vital truth: we can't justify our way into existence. We can't apologize for being. We can't duck away from the fearful shadows nor shrink from our inner light.

I had formed my initial story based on the circumstances of my early years. When I chose to recognize the authority of my own authorship, my life began to change.

We are the stories our souls are composing.

We needn't rip out pages, though we certainly have the authority to rewrite any chapter that no longer fits. We are on the path of *becoming* our selves. A journey that is sometimes delightful, sometimes overwhelming, but oh, what a ride.

There are times, I assure you, when we all feel a bit lost. These stories of ours are a marvel of complexity and are forever evolving. Sometimes life definitely feels like speculative fiction (What if I become *this?*). *Dare I explore my craving for art or music? What happens if I travel to Italy on my own or hike that mountain trail?*

Obviously we're all delicious mysteries (The Baffling Case of Who We Want to Be), and so much more. Even better, we're adventure stories. The map we follow leads us to the greatest treasure anyone could imagine. We become fully our Selves. Listen, dear friend, for clues the universe scatters about. The plot thickens. We've gotten so caught up in the story we forget whose internal hand pens this intricate tale.

It is your soul whispering provocative hints. For you and your soul are composing this life together. We are the heroes. It's now time for us to seize a pen and write a new chapter.

SUGGESTED FOCUS:

Imagine yourself as a fictional character. If you have a beloved tale from a movie or book, graphic novel or animated flick, even a cartoon from your childhood, who would you be? How would you insert yourself into that world?

Now imagine your current life is also a story. Imagine a pleasing plot twist. It can be an unexpected diversion or a change of scene. Infuse your 'story' with emotion and let yourself feel the pleasure of your new choice. Allow yourself to dwell on the potential within your imagined adventure.

Consider your own background as a story. What lessons did the heroine learn? How can you encourage her towards a new chapter?

AFFIRMATION: I am the author of my life story. I have the power of choice and I choose to be my own hero.

REVIEW:

As you practice examining your background as if it were a story, consider your favorite movies, books, or television shows. Which characters do you identify with and which ones set you on edge?

Within the fictional world, archetypes of characters are often straightforward. There is the cut-up, the hapless character who cracks jokes and provides comic relief (often at their own expense). The hero who struggles to find love or success. The maverick that breaks the rules. The successful one or the nerdy one or the ambitious one. The plucky heroine or the helpless waif.

Write a list of your favorite shows/movies/books along with the characters you identify with and the 'villains' you despise. Look for common themes. Those themes are a clue to the stories you have unconsciously adopted.

For an example, one of my favorite themes is the lonely girl who finds not just love but a family, as portrayed in the movie: "While You Were Sleeping."

Lucy rescues a man who falls into a coma. The family mistakenly believes she is their son's fiancée and welcomes her into the fold. It's so warm and cozy she's reluctant to confess the truth which would end the fantasy, and then she finds herself falling in love with Coma Boy's brother.

Towards the end, Lucy explains, "The truth was that I fell in love with you. Yes, all of you. I went from being all alone to being a fiancée, a daughter, a granddaughter, a sister, and a friend. I may have saved your life that day, but you really saved mine. You let me be a part of your family. I haven't had that in a really long time."

There was my fantasy, wrapped up with a beautiful bow: She found a family.

More uncomfortably, I vaguely remember a movie viewed as a kid, flickering on my old black and white television: "Where The Boys Are." A few years back, it rolled around on a cable channel and curious, I rewatched it. The character that previously had caught my attention, with whom I'd identified at the time, was someone who didn't think she was pretty and ended up being treated quite cruelly by a boy during their vacation. That shocked and saddened me, as I could remember feeling her pain as somehow heroic. I decided then and there to switch allegiance and instead imagine myself as the startlingly beautiful heroine who was also conveniently quite rich. The irony is such a switch stirs up emotions and forces us to break through our familiar stories and write new plot lines.

As you go through your list, consider how it would **feel** *to switch focus and identify with another character. Write down the emotions that arise.*

Ask yourself: How would my life be different if I acted like This Character instead of That One?

Consider jotting down how your past choices might have differed had you thought of yourself as That Character. What choices might you have made? Who would you have liked? Who would you have wanted to become?

TEN
THE NEW NORMAL

There is just one life for each of us: our own.

EURIPIDES

What exactly does it mean to be normal?

I peered out through the smudged lens of my childhood experiences, assuming the tidy homes of my classmates reflected some mysterious ideal. Homes with two parents and tasty home-cooked meals. Pot roast on Sundays, cold glasses of chocolate milk and home-baked oatmeal cookies after school. Homes with matching towels and freshly mowed lawns reflected a sense of order I'd never experienced.

Like a shy kitten, I'd edge my way into the homes of my friends. Kitchens with shiny floors and snacks for hungry children, colorful curtains and polished furniture. In retrospect I now realize every family had their shadows, but to me just the absence of strife and the neatly made beds were as strangely wondrous as the yellow brick road in my beloved Oz.

That must be what normal is, my younger self mused.

Normal was definitely not something I could attribute to my personal corner of the universe. Not in a perpetually messy house where an indifferent mother rebelled against parental obligations. Not with tangled sheets, unwashed dishes, a house empty of supervision. Definitely not with a parent who preferred midnight drinks with coworkers to coming home to read bedtime stories to her fatherless children.

Normality—the benchmark—played out in TV shows before my time. Shows like *Father Knows Best, Leave It To Beaver,* and *The Brady Bunch* portrayed happy families with easily resolved problems and cozy relationships. In the earliest years, I related more to the old Shirley Temple movies flickering in black and white on our small television. A remnant of fables left over from World War II, when it was vital to give children an emotional grasp of what it meant to be orphaned, either by one parent or even by both. This was the life with which I numbly identified. A life of struggle and chaos, where pennies were counted and wishes left unfulfilled.

In the 60's, my widowed mother of three struggled, not just to make ends meet, but to raise desperately lonely children who were a graphic, irritating reminder of the husband she had passionately loved and abruptly lost.

We certainly didn't have cozy family dinners or special traditions. I made do with mushy bowls of cereal and cold sandwiches. Canned spaghetti sauce with jack cheese toasted on white bread or macaroni with hot dogs were considered a special treat (and they were!). I earned cash by creating popsicles: pouring grape Kool-Aid into an ice cube tray and carefully placing toothpicks into each square while partially frozen. I'd lug my cooler down to Johnny's Market and hang out in front of the store, offering up my wares to anyone who'd buy. Other times, I dragged my brother's discarded red wagon to the homes of neighbors, begging for soda bottles to return, all with the intent of saving up those nickels to buy a foil-wrapped burger at the local arcade.

Mom's relations with her own siblings were uneasy and distant. Raised in the Depression era when a woman's primary role revolved around birthing and raising children, her desire to be an independent woman was an anomaly. Back then, a woman's duty was to provide abundant offspring. The limits of modern medicine of the time meant not every baby grew to adulthood.

A few of her siblings died in their childhood. The eldest sister was twelve when my mother was born. Being the youngest in a large family meant she fought for scraps of attention. Competition is often a means of survival for lonely children, a sad dynamic that would emerge within our family as well. Mom hated the idea of being trapped in the same sort of servitude that she perceived in her mother's life. Being married was an escape of sorts. Yet clearly raising children was not a joyful or fulfilling choice but rather a distraction that had to be tolerated.

Based on her actions, her desire was not to foster a loving family but to dodge the nuisance and hardship of being the only adult responsible for our care. In retrospect I could understand her frustration. She imagined herself as a dashing heroine, a pioneering female, a woman of adventure and success. Her childhood wasn't easy either. Even with two parents, being raised during the Depression in a time when women were expected to marry young and follow a proscribed path meant she felt trapped and desperate for change.

During World War II, women were encouraged to step into roles left empty by the enlistment of so many eligible soldiers. My mom was hired to be a riveter in California during the last years of the war. She found her niche—intricate assembly done at record speed, a challenge she took on and mastered. Mom did so well, she was selected to mentor other young women embracing a job that became memorialized through the icon: Rosie the Riveter.

Still in her late teens, she flew off to Chicago to train new hires. It was a heady time for her, an era of independence she never forgot. Bunking with several young women close to her own age, thriving on the frenzy of work each day, then pooling pennies to grab Chinese takeout to share after hours, those were the memories she would confide with a wistful sigh. Fast-paced, thrilling times a few years prior to my dad, whom she'd eventually meet and within two days marry. As the youngest, her secret fear was that she'd be stuck caring for her parents while her elder sisters lived full and productive lives. What she desperately yearned to do instead was attend college, study and learn. Be...something.

Her parents had different plans for their youngest daughter. Either marry, or return and live at home to be the dedicated daughter who'd care for them as the years went by.

Dad must have seemed like the answer to an unspoken prayer. He adored her, she adored him. When he traveled to business conferences, she traveled along, her purse full of wifely remedies for stomach ailments and headaches for his fellow salesmen far from the comforts of home. She was his smart and pretty wife, more of a partner than a housewife. It took four years to get pregnant, and when she did, everything changed. Her dream would be postponed, they agreed, until the kids were in school. The day he died, that dream shattered.

With an emotionally distant mom, my only true sense of family came from the handful of glorious summers we were shipped off to our grandparent's summer cabin at a lake in New Jersey. Those idyllic days had to sustain me; coupled with whatever insight I could glean from watching unrealistically cheery TV families.

The Brady Bunch first arrived in 1969, with a twist on the typical homey sitcom family. Mr. Brady was a widower, and Mrs. Brady's former husband? They never quite answered that question. Yet the premise was sound for those kids struggling to find hope within a world where couples divorced or a parent unaccountably vanished from our lives. The father worked, the mother stayed home, and good old Alice did the cooking and cleaning. Even better for this lonely girl, the siblings and stepsiblings bonded, watched out for each other, working together as a family in a way I'd never experienced.

Mom and Dad Brady needed money? The kids would work as a team to figure out the solution. What a concept. Corny and goofy but heartwarming to watch as this made-up family acted out the fantasy of what normality must be. Potato-sack races and homemade sack lunches.

And this crew must somehow form a family, that's the way we all became the Brady Bunch.

Scripted relationships filled the empty space within my aching heart.

Perhaps my own sense of identity would have flourished if we had at least settled in one home. Mom was restless. A psychological nomad. Landlords were another symbol of authority to rebel against.

It seems as if we moved constantly. At least eighteen moves before I even hit age fifteen—how could a vulnerable child develop any sense of continuity? Much less develop an identity more substantial than the tissue-thin sense of self I was left to clutch.

The solution for me may be a familiar tale to anyone who lives life feeling like an outsider. It is then we unconsciously decide *not* fitting in would be the go-to identity.

Rebellion would fill the hole where self-esteem belonged.

Being near-sighted and too insecure to wear glasses until my teens meant I couldn't even catch a hesitant smile, which might have indicated a potential chum. My world of blurriness nullified any distinctive edges, which left it up to me to provide the definition my life demanded. Identifying with the misfits or rebels became an easy call. Especially for a child with no inkling of who she is *supposed* to be.

Entering junior high, I encountered teachers predisposed to judge me based on the misbehavior of my older siblings. To my fragile ego, they seemed to take pleasure in assuming my performance and behavior would match their biased perception. With my ironically eager-to-please yearning to live up to outer expectations (no matter how destructive), I obliged by being the fuck-up they wanted to believe in.

Unrealistic in retrospect and yet very telling.

How often do we make these unconscious choices? Those who lack a distinct sense of identity, who face bitterly challenging or harrowing circumstances in youth, often develop increased empathy. A compensation and survival mechanism that allows us to sense what will procure the acceptance so desperately craved.

The irony for me is to recognize there is absolutely no standard for normality. Like so many others, my yearning was simply a wispy fantasy I chased, one without hope of a happily-ever-after. While investing in a measure of conformity to society's expectations could provide a meager sense of security and comfort, it's a dubious proposition. Rarely does it provide the pay-off our emotional yearning seeks. The idealistic view of the blandly contented family with no actual challenges, so beautifully portrayed in neatly scripted sit-coms, doesn't actually exist, except within a clever writer's imagination. In a world where even the most perplexing situation, the most outrageous predicaments can be neatly resolved in a half-hour, we learn very little. Instead of life lessons, we compensate by applying a colorful bandage around an inner wound, which requires true healing.

I fell madly in love with the stories by Edward Eager, starting with *Half-Magic*. Written before my time, they were set even farther back in history, when cars were just appearing on deserted highways and Flappers were a thing. The author was born in 1911, so the time period of the roaring twenties correlated to his own childhood. The kids in his books were gratifyingly realistic. Rather than the plastic perfection of the Brady Bunch, they were ordinary children with faults a'plenty. Not only that, they struggled with a similar theme, as the father has died before the first book begins, leaving a widowed mother working hard to support her family.

In the first book, the rash, impatient, and forthright eldest girl, Jane, scoops up a nickel from a crack in the sidewalk not realizing what she casually tossed into her pocket is actually a magic talisman. Her leadership skills will be challenged and eventually honed, thanks to the unexpected mishaps-turned-adventures within these pages. Similar to just about every book that captured my attention, the kids had wild adventures and of course, struggled to understand themselves and each other. The perfect series of books to inspire the philosophy that would eventually become my life's journey: the circumstances of life are designed to teach us how to become our greatest self.

Like Harry Potter would do in later years, they faced trials and tribulations that were often harrowing. By meeting those mythical challenges head-on, the fictional heroes discovered how the qualities arising from testing themselves are the foundation of identity. *This is what it means to be a person*, I realized. To stand up, to strive, to discover, and to *become* your Self.

It wasn't about potato sack races at all, it was about self-awareness and growth.

Maybe my struggle to feel loved in an empty house or to

shore up my courage not to quake in fear when left alone too late at night wasn't the same as standing up to dastardly pirates or evil magicians. Yet it is through the mythical struggles that we experience a release. I couldn't stand up and face down the real "monster" in the form of a violent stepfather, but by visualizing myself slaying an imaginary dragon with a cookbook of spells and a good dose of humor, I felt stronger, more assured, and this helped me to awaken my own inner hero.

I suspect many people share the same sense of doubt that plagued me as a child. For some, perhaps, it's a passing shadow rather than a crippling infirmity. Others like me may have struggled to see even a faint glimmer of reassuring light. Those who hide from their shadows have the most debilitating struggle of all. They are often the souls who seem the most put together. They are the ones who tuck away their fears with rigid care, thrusting the shadows out of sight from others, but most especially from their own scrutiny.

It feels at times like an endless journey, this path to knowing and becoming our selves. A path as dangerously rocky as it is bright with hope. Sometimes it feels as if we stumble over stones strewn carelessly about, or placed with malicious design to prevent our progress. Yet in truth, those obstacles serve an invaluable purpose. Without even realizing it, we instinctively swerve to find them, to help trip up our tendency to ignore the harder truths. Pausing to examine those seemingly random pebbles is how we find true clarity. How else to force ourselves to recognize we're stumbling in the dark? How else to discover hiding from the light of consciousness makes it easier to ignore the shadows, but keeps us forever trapped in an unconscious state?

Today I'd like to send positive energy to you. I salute your bravery, your strength, your courage, and your determination. I acknowledge the pain you've endured, the sorrowful tears you've hidden, and even the mortification that can be inevitable when at last we dare to face a piercing reflection in the mirror. More than anything thank you for moving forward, one day, one revelation at a time. Every step you take is a step towards awareness. Every act of courageously examining your beliefs, facing your judgments, and releasing your pain, is an act of courage, which helps to awaken and heal not just you, but our entire world.

Thank you.

SUGGESTED FOCUS:

Take one incident from your past that severely challenged you. Imagine it as a fictional event. What lessons might the author have intended? What qualities of being emerged as result of your tribulations?

Now visualize you as the author sending encouragement and support to you as the character. "I'm so proud of you! Look at how far you've come. You are a Hero."

AFFIRMATION: I am the hero of my own life. I am constantly supported and encouraged by my inner self.

REVIEW:

Write down a list of your fictional heroes and heroines, along with your favorite stories—books, television shows, comics, or movies. Next to each hero or heroine, jot down the character traits that you identify with, as well as any traits that you find uncomfortable.

Although I identified with Harry Potter due to my challenging childhood and feeling unwanted, a friend assumed I would most identify with Hermione. Was it because he thought me to be bossy or a know-it-all or a quick learner? It triggered me a bit and yet upon reflection I began to appreciate the comparison. I have great leadership skills, have a wide range of knowledge and do tend to be a quick learner. Why should that bother me? Owning those qualities helped me to realize that I'd been judging Me, just as Hermione felt judged by her friends in the Harry Potter series.

Next to your list of favorite stories, explore which themes are most prevalent. My themes are often about finding or forming a family of friends, discovering inner strength, and identifying and becoming my truest self. Which themes stand out for you?

This list is a glimpse of your own personal mythic journey. The heroes and heroines you admire, the challenges they overcame, and their quests are reflecting your journey.

In fairy tales and mythical fables the fairy godmother or wise wizard may assist our young hero. In mystical explorations, we may yearn for a compassionate, all-knowing Oversoul to encourage us and help us grow.

Here's one of our secret powers.

You and I can be that oversoul.

In one aspect, we're the eager, hopeful hero who sometimes stumbles and needs counsel. In another aspect, we're the wise, kind, compassionate, thoughtful oversoul whose precious light guides our questing souls. When we take on the role of being our own oversoul, an amazing turn of events slips into place. We set up a pattern of listening, along with a pattern of being the voice within. The more we practice this, the easier and more powerful the voice becomes.

Now place yourself in the role of an oversoul or fairy godmother or wise magician or ancient shaman. Take one of your personal memories and fictionalize it. Write it out as if it were a story, but this time, insert changes. Step into the story as the over-

soul, either within a dream or a magical setting. Create at least one alternate ending that brings you relief or pleasure or a sense of resolution. Consider how this journey is now a mythic tale and you can write it out exactly as you choose.

Let yourself explore the emotions that arise with your new ending(s).

ELEVEN
WHO DO I THINK I AM?

My life has been long, and believing that life loves the liver of it, I have dared to try many things, sometimes trembling, but daring, still.

MAYA ANGELOU, LETTER TO MY
DAUGHTER

When I was a child, a common phrase was, "Who do you think you are?"

These were words heard directly or implied by manner or tone by many of the adults in my childhood. Anytime there was a yearning to speak up for myself or say, "No," the message was clear: *know your place and stick to it.*

When I hesitantly told my mom that I wanted to shop for a bra, my stepfather snorted with derision, *"Who do you think you are?"* As I was still a preteen, he wanted me to know that I didn't qualify for womanhood. Nor did I have the right to be *anything* without his specific approval.

Sometimes it's classmates pretending to be friends who challenge us for daring to step outside of the accepted circle of accomplishment. *"You* want to audition for the lead?"

Or family members who want to remind you of the pecking order and where you belong. "Don't think you're better than us!"

In later life it may be a lover or an overbearing supervisor who uses thinly veiled contempt to crush our spirit or keep us under emotional lock-down.

These words are often delivered as an edgy dare, a scornful sneer, or with a distinct undertone of sinister warning. A hint we are expected to act in a very specific way. We are to neatly confine ourselves in an acceptable box and conform to all expectations—whether spoken or implied. We are taught to never, ever consider challenging (with our behavior or our words) the stated comfort zone.

Many of us take this admonishment to heart, rigorously applying it to our own life. Oh, in time we may learn how to tentatively nibble vegetables we avoided as children. We might release qualms and thrill ourselves with adrenalin-producing adventures. Yet many of us at one point in our early years drew a line around the perimeter of our personality and silently stated: *this is where I belong.*

Our comfort zone.

Of course, comfort is not where growth originates.

A seedling breaking through the soil, the fledgling bird pecking with determination through the shell, the caterpillar transforming into the glorious butterfly: these are not examples of comfort but a provocative summons, beckoning us towards an irrevocable transformation.

We delight in the beauty of the butterfly, but rarely admit the changes it has gone through to achieve that beauty. — Maya Angelou

Our discomfort zone is where any meaningful change occurs.

It is there where our hidden dreams are feverishly plotted out, where our burning motivation is kindled with bright hopes and flames of desire.

Who do you think you are?

There is indeed a daring challenge in those words. Sometimes an admonishment we not "get above ourselves." The latter phrase always reminds me of my childhood days, lost in reverie within the Greek and Roman myths of old. Silly humans aspiring to taste the glory of Mt. Olympus. The famous "Tower of Babel," where humans possessed the audacity to craft a tremendous tower with the intention of reaching the level of the Gods.

Hubris.

Believing better of yourself than one really should.

The other night, I reveled in a brilliant film, *Hidden Figures*.

It's 1961.

The Soviet Union has successfully launched a man into space. The United States is determined to not only do the same, but one better. Orbiting Earth will be the first step, with the ultimate goal of landing on the moon.

Before computers took over, a team of people was required to handle the myriad complicated mathematical calculations necessary for any large-scale scientific project. During that time, mathematician Katherine Goble worked as a human computer at Langley Research Center in Hampton, Virginia, along with her colleagues, Mary Jackson (an aspiring engineer) and their 'unofficial' acting supervisor, Dorothy Vaughan. The department was rigidly segregated, both by gender and race. NASA focused on the task at hand—to launch our first astronaut into space. This feat would require stringent calculations. Given Ms. Goble's masterful skills in analytic geometry, she was assigned to assist Al Harrison's Space Task group. This made her the first black woman on the team.

During this time period, women could barely get approval for their intelligence or skills and a woman of color was rarely tolerated, much less respected. For a male to accept that a woman, particularly one of a different race, could be superior in intellect or skill was unimaginable. Yet in the end, it was Katherine who successfully created the equation that guided the space capsule during re-entry, allowing it to return safely home. As frequently happened during this time period, her accomplishment was not credited and her name was removed from the official reports.

She and her colleagues struggled not only to be respected, but to accomplish stellar achievements beyond the scope of our imagination. In 2015, Katherine received the Presidential Medal of Freedom and the next year NASA dedicated a building at Langley Research Center in her honor.

The movie depicted a time strictly dominated by Caucasian men. This was an age when women, and especially minorities, were firmly expected to not ever even dare to step outside the invisible lines drawn by those who presumed to be their betters. A time when brilliant African American women leapt above the expectations and capabilities of those who insisted on their own superiority. Their unparalleled achievements made an impact that changed our world, even if it would be decades before they were given their due.

Katherine, Mary, and Dorothy all dared to challenge the unreasonable boundaries imposed by the racism and sexism of their times. They successfully broke barriers, and though it would be too many years before their achievements could be acknowledged, they kicked open metaphorical doors for women and minorities alike.

Should you or I dare to reach for our own stars? To stretch

beyond the limits imposed by our own trembling fear or by the admonishments of others?

One risk I took was to reach beyond the gravitational pull of my own background. Gazing in awe at those who played music with such ease, I wondered what would be the point in even trying. When my sister first encountered a guitar, she picked it up, restrung it with seeming ease, tuned the strings and immediately began writing songs. Me? I struggled to play a C chord, then an F, then a D, allowing me to clumsily strum an old favorite classic rock tune.

Her raw talent inspired me but her attitude towards my fumbling efforts echoed the sentiment first heard so long ago: *Who do you think you are?*

As the decades rolled past, my determination took me much farther than her raw talent and now there are hundreds of songs that I can play with ease. I've taken the stage a few times over the years and can hold my own without fear or doubts. I dared, and that led me to countless nights of pleasure and satisfaction.

Whether the accomplishment launches the capsule that allows the first human to plant a flag on the moon or it allows us to soar past our own fears, it's a tremendous feat. So…

Let us dare.

Let us dare to breathe in hope, to speak with passion, and to dream our selves into being.

SUGGESTED FOCUS:

What would you do or who would you be if there were no limits whatsoever? There are theories that every probability that can exist does, so why not create our own? Envision an alternate path of your life, one where you explore the road not taken, whether from childhood or yesterday. It could be a career you considered or a town that appealed. Is there a yearning to create or perform, to explore new lands or learn a new language?

Imagine yourself following that alternate path, from any point in your personal history. The "you" who took up painting in your teens or went to a new country in your twenties. Imagine reaching out to that other "you" and connecting on an inner level. Imagine tapping into "her" talents, skill, education, or experience. Remind yourself that imagination can be more powerful than we have ever realized. Quantum Physics suggests all worlds that can exist, do. Open the doors to the greater self and see what she can teach us.

AFFIRMATION: <u>*The knowledge and experience of all my probabilities is available to me. I open myself up to experience all I can be.*</u>

REVIEW:

Pick one or two of the paths not taken: whether it was to be a rock star or a physician, an astronaut or a teacher, an artist or a lawyer. Write your choice at the top of the page, along with a date (whether precise or approximate).

Write a short bio or journal entry from the point of view of your other probability. For example, my initial studies in psychology as a teen had me considering the possibility of becoming a psychologist. However my paralyzing insecurities were such that I couldn't conceive of myself in such a masterful role. Although I studied independently, that was a path not chosen. Yet today I can tap into "her" wisdom and analytical ability. By imagining her professional status, I can also gain strength and even a sense of inner authority.

Another example would be my fervent desire to be an actress, a path I explored briefly in my twenties. Ultimately, it didn't suit me (though I certainly had fun while it lasted) yet "her" ability to step forth into the spotlight with confidence can be brought forth into my own personality.

This exercise has no limits. You can explore as many alternate paths as you choose or expand the bio into a longer story. What did "she" accomplish? Did "he" move to a different area? What might you learn from her if you were to sit down together for a cup of tea? What insight might he offer about the road not taken?

TWELVE
CREATING A NEW BACKSTORY

We do not need magic to change the world. We carry all the power we need inside ourselves already: we have the power to imagine better.

J.K ROWLING, *HARVARD COMMENCEMENT SPEECH*

Beliefs are such tricky things. We perceive them as reality with a capital R, an undeniable fact with indisputable proof.

Reality.

Doesn't matter if those seemingly solid beliefs can be altered, sometimes in the twinkling of the eye, other times requiring a bit more effort. Beliefs can *feel* as substantial as a solidly built brick wall. When a belief is locked into place, contrary facts or outer circumstances have no impact. We build a foundation with the piles of beliefs we've gathered throughout our life.

I am strong; I am weak.

People love me; people hate me.
I talk too much; I never speak up.

Pick up a marshmallow and toss it against your wall of beliefs and see what a dent you make. We don't realize the belief-bricks can be swapped out for other belief-bricks, which will then be just as substantial. We construct our life like a house built on beliefs, with windows of perception.

I discovered this insight in my teens, yet it took me years to develop the awareness to put it into practice.

One of the first philosophical axioms to challenge my root assumptions still clicks, the Glass Half-Empty metaphor: *The glass is either half-full or half-empty, depending on how you perceive it.*

Hmmm... At first the notion simply danced in my thoughts, then one day at school up in the wintery mountains, I saw it play out. The weather station predicted a storm and that morning, chomping on cold cereal, my ears were glued to the radio, hoping to hear an announcement that school would be closed. Unfortunately my wish did not come true. So like every other kid in my class, I trudged up to the bus stop.

While I waited for the bus early on that frigid morning, a few flakes drifted down, powdering everything with fine fluff. I played around making snow-prints until the bus arrived and we climbed up the steps, jostling for position and headed to school.

Listening to the teacher talk, we could barely pay attention as we kept glancing out the frosty window, anticipating our wintery fun when class let out. An hour or so later, the weather shifted and huge clumps of descending snowflakes filled the sky. We all watched with eager anticipation as the snow quickly piled up. Excitement rippled through my class. We could already imagine grabbing our sleds and soaring down the snow-laden hills.

The decision was made to close the school early and send us

home while the busses could still navigate roads. Practically jumping up and down, I snatched up my books, hurried into my coat and ran to the bus. A couple of classmates grumbled. "Why didn't they just close the school this morning? Then we'd have the whole day."

That thought had never even occurred to me! I was just so thrilled to have a half-day of exuberant fun. It actually boggled the mind to perceive what struck me as good fortune, instead as a disappointment. To them the day was half-empty, yet for me it was half-full of delicious opportunities to romp in a winter wonderland.

As the years drifted by, delightful sayings continued to pop up on my path, like bright butterflies dancing around my budding optimistic self.

Clouds with silver linings populated my inner sky.

This was close to a decade before I opened my mind to the concept of how beliefs shape our perception, along with our self-image. Understanding that life is a mirror, reflecting back the inner shadows we fear and the light we embrace, has changed my life. It started with me recognizing the value of looking at the bright side of life, and understanding how seeking out the sunshine among the clouds meant I'd be deliberately choosing a brighter path.

Over the years I began to realize how many similarly optimistic people yearned to break free from patterns of doubt and fear. They'd confide their deep-rooted worries and share carefully worded positive affirmations. A good start but not necessarily the ultimate power-tool required to rearrange those building blocks of belief.

Why is that?

What we rarely consider is how we form identities around the beliefs we choose: identities as colorful and substantial as our favorite characters in books and films. Not only do we form personalities, we automatically create backstories, which may be based on actual events in our probable past or may simply be a distorted perception based on emotional bias. Meaning, our emotions paint a picture and we then believe what this picture tells us is true. The memories *feel* substantial and provide a foundation for whichever beliefs we have chosen, either consciously or unconsciously, to embrace.

"*I am ugly.*"

There was one of my core beliefs. From a very early age, too.

There was no real basis for a belief I accepted as fact. It wasn't based on mirrors because ironically my sight was too poor to see myself clearly. Yet it was a belief I adopted and one that I found reflected back to me, if only by the attitudes of others.

One major factor was my mom's own beliefs, as is so often the case with children. She didn't think much of outer beauty. Being somewhat intellectual, she scorned women in pretty dresses and heels. In retrospect, of course I could see it was a defense mechanism, a shield she could wield against her fear others would scorn her, that perhaps she wasn't "pretty enough." She'd make off-hand comments about my sister's attractiveness (somehow a less desirable trait) and others would like *me* for more substantial reasons. In actuality, my mother really was quite pretty, unconventional with a Katherine Hepburn flair.

However she told me often that I was like *Sarah, Plain and Tall*, the heroine in a children's book by Patricia MacLachlan, later made into a movie. Rather than reassuring, this was a reference that stung. She would reference my sister as being pretty while saying that I was attractive in a "different way." It didn't help that we had little money for new clothes, and would travel a half-hour down the mountain to paw through the racks at the Salvation Army thrift store. When I'd wistfully gaze at pretty coats with fluffy fake fur collars, she'd practically sneer, then exclaim how she hated those kind of coats. *"I always wanted one of those big yellow slickers, wouldn't that be great?"*

Um... no, but as a child, I rarely spoke up about my own needs much less my fervent desires. Her attitude made it clear: wanting pretty things (like my fourteen-year-old sister did) was shallow. Like it or not, whether I agreed or not, my role was to believe that my mother and I were somehow the same. Therefore I should scorn pretty things like fashionable coats or attractive boots and prefer yellow rain slickers and clunky galoshes.

I still remember with a painful twinge in fourth grade when my two best friends said, "Let's swap coats for the day!"

Eagerly, I chimed in, "I'll swap too!"

They looked at each other for a long moment and then, avoiding my eyes, said, "Um, that's okay."

Ouch.

Now here's where the idea of memory gets tricky. The book I referenced, *Sarah, Plain and Tall,* wasn't actually written until I was an adult. It became popular years after I could finally afford to choose my own winter coat. Yet as I typed up a snippet of my background, my mind pulled it up as a reference with a clear memory of my mom saying this *when I was a child*. A few minutes later, I wondered and jumped on the internet to research the title.

My nagging suspicion about my memory turned up a surprise. When Mom did actually reference the book, it was over a decade after I was grown. Granted, she affirmed regularly, outer beauty was not desirable and a quality to be scorned. Along with a pointed reminder I should be proud because I was certainly no beauty. So... it's still part of my "back story" apparently, and my memory pieced together two events to provide a "fact" to serve a childhood belief. It didn't happen in my childhood, but I inserted a memory of it there because it supported my back story.

That's how it works.

Every freaking time.

The past is alive. Although linear time is real enough, it's also an illusion. The past lives on, just as the future is active way before our perception catches up.

People cling to beliefs and create substantial memories to justify them.

We could just as easily plant new beliefs and create probable memories to justify those. Psychological studies have proven repeatedly implanted memories have as much of an impact on our belief system as (so-called) real memories.

What you believe is what you become.

"I am beautiful."

Here's how it works. I can conjure up a new memory to create a flood of positive emotions. This memory can help me to create a new backstory. I can utilize self-hypnosis or a light trance state to help provide a receptive framework for my newly chosen self-image based on a newly created backstory.

<u>We can create new memories that will provide emotional support and satisfaction.</u>

It's rather like the pleasure we get from watching a favorite sitcom, or sinking into the plot of a familiar beloved book. Through our imagination, we slip into the persona of those characters we adore, and *feel* their emotions. Those felt emotions lift our hearts or make us weep. When we relate to the characters, like my mom apparently did with the book she referenced, the emotional impact affects us in a similar way to the memories we choose to recall. Mom related to the heroine in the story so the plot line empowered her, and she assumed it would empower me as well. It may well have except that was her story, not mine.

<u>*Our past is like a memorized plot line supporting our current self-image.*</u>

So if I choose, I can create imaginary plot lines to support my new belief or my new self-image. Instead of reinforcing a belief that my appearance is unattractive by dredging up real (or imaginary) memories, I can choose to create an alternate story to support an alternate belief.

New belief: *I am as beautiful as a fresh daisy.*

Now I'll create a story to be an alternate memory—a new plot line that leads to a different perspective of who I imagine myself to be.

Here's my story:

I remember when my mom laughed and handed me a daisy she plucked from a crack in the sidewalk. "This is beautiful," she said, "just like you. And every wish you make fills your inner sky with hopes and dreams which turn into stars to guide you through life."

This glorious little snippet can now be a new "memory." And it's just as emotionally viable as any other snippet. The more I consider it, the more I imagine it, the more substantial this memory will become. This is a proven technique. Moreover, we do this all the time without realizing it. We hand-select memories from every encounter, every moment. We shape them and color them and infuse them with emotion. Then, those intense emotions from our chosen memories sustain all of our beliefs. The beliefs we have chosen unconsciously only have power until we bring them into the light of consciousness and choose to replace them with new and improved beliefs.

Which beliefs should I choose? Which ones will you choose?

Here's one new belief for you: *I can be whoever I choose to be. I hold within me the power to change my mental focus and change my life.*

Starting right now, this can be a new belief. And I will help you remember.

. . .

SUGGESTED FOCUS:

Pick an unproductive belief you wish to change. In the chapter above, we used my belief about my appearance, but it can be any belief that holds you back.

"I'm not worthy of..." "I always fail." "People don't like me." Find a memory that supports that belief. Tell yourself "That memory is just a story. The story can be changed."

Reframe the belief. "I'm worthy of..." "I can and do succeed." "People appreciate me." Now, create a new memory that supports that belief. Be patient if this is challenging at first. There may be resistance because the old belief is so ingrained. Persist. You can do it.

Explore the idea of an alternate past, knowing that in a world of endless probabilities, we can choose to create and then focus on a more fulfilling past.

AFFIRMATION: *The past is just a memory and memories change all the time. Knowing this, I create and choose memories that support the best me I can imagine.*

REVIEW:

Choose one (or more) of the reframed beliefs. For example, changing the belief, "People don't appreciate or respect me," to "People really do appreciate and respect me," will stir up feelings and perhaps trigger fears because beliefs become part of our identity. Write down the emotions that arise. Examine your list, then write a letter to the part of your being that needs reassurance.

"Dear younger me, I believe in you!"

Write from the point of view of being the 'older' self, the future self, the one who has the answers. This exercise can be not only cathartic, many find it prompts a connection to an inner voice just waiting in the wings.

Now refocus on your changed belief. "People really do appreciate and respect me," Imagine the probable You who is now emerging as a result of this altered focus. Let yourself examine the emotions of the probable self that you are now becoming. Write a brief note from the viewpoint of this probable self.

"People appreciate and respect me, and it's so fun now to meet up at gatherings. I enjoy the conversations and have such a great time!"

THIRTEEN
BE TRUE TO YOUR SELF

We are so accustomed to disguise ourselves to others that in the end we become disguised to ourselves.

FRANÇOIS VI DE LA ROCHEFOUCAULT

When I was in third grade, my first foray into independence began with selling Girl Scout cookies door-to-door. I enjoyed trotting up to my neighbor's homes, proud of the responsibility. Attention was also something I desperately craved so the acceptance and kindness from adults when they answered the door was immensely gratifying. When I eagerly trudged up a hilly slope to one door, I didn't notice the hand-lettered cardboard sign pounded into the ground until it was too late.

Beware of the dog.

Ferocious barking didn't have time to register before the German Shepherd leaped, pinning me to the ground. I felt the pain in my arm, saw the snapping jaws and wide eyes of the savagely fierce creature, wrenched myself up and staggered down the hill. In shock, I cradled my left arm with my other hand, staggering up and down that tiny street, calling out in a weak voice, "Help me, help me, somebody please help me."

No one came.

My mother at work, my siblings off with their friends. Why didn't a single neighbor peer out their window? Was there no curiosity about an eight-year-old stumbling down the lane with blood dripping down her arm?

Finally the dog owner himself came out, sheepishly, I'm sure. He brought me up to his place, wrapped the bleeding arm and scowled, telling me repeatedly that *there was a sign.*

Eventually, my mom came home from work and dragged me off to the doctor who told me dispassionately that the dog probably just wanted to warn me. "Had he actually bitten you, he would have taken off your arm."

Oddly, that made sense. That poor dog, chained to a pole, trapped in a lonely life without love. Left out continuously, I realized later, throughout the long nights and endless days. He never barked except that one time when I crossed the perimeter. Not affectionately cherished as a family pet, this dog was meant only to serve as an alarm system for his owner. He stayed hidden in the shadows, barely visible unless you approached. After the incident, I'd cautiously go past the house, peering up at the dog who peered back down just as solemnly. There was no anger, though the fear still made me quake.

When I was a child, I too felt invisible.

It's not something that can be easily explained by a singular event. I can point to the fact that my siblings were four and six years older, garnering the lion's share of attention. When my dad was alive, he was apparently outgoing and amiable. Being comfortable and friendly in social situations helped him become the top salesman, then Director, West Coast Sales at Anheuser-Busch. Mom told me that after every business trip, Dad would come home with his pockets stuffed with phone numbers of 'new friends.' One of the rare photos that remains from my childhood shows my siblings and mom laughing uproariously with my dad. He was the affectionate one. A handful of photos documenting our life with Dad reveal a loving father that I barely remember. I see him teaching my sister how to ride a bike, or helping us onto the swing set. From all accounts, my mom was content to let my father be the nurturing one.

Piecing together fragments of the few memories I could get from my mom, I was the anomaly, and instead tucked myself away unlike my bolder siblings and jovial dad. Shy around strangers though I also remember being bold enough as a toddler to dance around with great enthusiasm whenever music wafted through the house.

It would be rational to assume that losing my doting father, being overwhelmed by the whirlwind of chaos of too many moves and too little affection, had a powerful impact. Mom's emphasis on the general lack of importance of her offspring sent a message straight to my psyche that my presence was of little significance.

Yet it also boils down to one simple psychological fact.

Emotional neglect often results in a child who believes she is not visible. She may be ignored, her needs overlooked, the caretaker may even actively avoid noticing the child for fear that any acknowledgement might necessitate action. The result of this neglect typically goes one way or the other. When over-attention turns to stark neglect, the offspring may tend towards narcissism and competition, like my siblings. When it is primarily neglect, they usually flip to the other side of the page.

They shut down, become numb.

Praise is craved yet rarely received. They're then drawn to those with gigantic personalities to compensate for their own tiny stature.

The neglected child can be especially attracted to narcissists who display the exaggerated confidence lacking in their extreme insecurity. They seek out those who will eventually treat them with the contempt and indifference they unconsciously believe is deserved.

So it wasn't who I actually was, but rather how I perceived myself. My sister was bold, sassy, and determined to get her way. She gleefully shared stories like how, at age six, she'd strolled to the local market, tossed her favorite treats into a cart and attempted to push it home. My brother and sister competed for attention, and for the most part, I was in awe of those around me.

Funny how perception works. There are those individuals who from the moment they rise precariously to toddle on their own two feet feel themselves to be larger than life. Oh, how I admired those with such dashing self-confidence, such brilliantly shining self-esteem. Souls with grand personalities of such stature their presence barely fit inside a room.

This was not me.

My sense of self could barely fit into a peanut shell—my confidence that easily shattered.

When we're children, our identity is often formed by observation. Either by observing those beings around us, or the characters in storybooks, movies, television shows, or in my case, animated cartoons.

The first character I truly felt a kinship with as a toddler was Casper the Friendly Ghost.

Telling, isn't it?

A flimsy wraith. Unsubstantial, and not quite of this world, yet with an instinct to be kind and friendly.

True to the psychology of being drawn to those who exhibit traits we yearn to own, I blindly worshiped those who displayed the qualities I lacked: audacity, self-confidence, an unwavering commitment to self-interest, and all with a streak of reckless disregard for consequence.

My sister was bold enough to take what she wanted. Her recklessness meant she'd dare us to crawl over the fence at the local arcade to jump on trampolines at night, urging us to join her. Heart pounding every time she shouted "Car," as we threw ourselves down flat to avoid the illuminating headlights. She'd persuade me to shoplift OTC drugs for her and my brother, and, believing that these were acts of courage (rather than recklessness), I'd eagerly comply. I didn't know better. Even worse, I didn't realize I deserved better than a role model who brought out the worst in me.

My belief that I deserved little was reinforced by my mom. When I was eight, I remember her buying electric blankets for my brother and sister to endure the cold winter nights.

"You don't need it," Mom informed me. "You're not selfish like your sister."

Somehow that made *selfish* seem both unsavory and highly appealing.

At fourteen, my yearning to be as confident as my dangerously inclined sister meant I'd seek out friends who reflected a similarly dubious character. I gasped in wonder at a friend who could lie with a straight face to just about anyone. To my childish view, this took a daring I couldn't imagine possessing.

In my quest to discover, explore, and eventually become my self, a curious shift happened. Despite my wild youth, my hunger was not to continue on a path of reckless abandon but to smooth out the edges, gain strength and wisdom.

I tamed myself and strove to unlock the patterns that chained me to my fears. Only then could I experience the freedom only self-confidence could offer. It would be awhile before I could perceive myself as anything more than a loyal pet to those who occasionally patted me on the head, but it was a start.

I still chuckle remembering how at the age of seventeen, I began. The goal was my first true commitment—to dedicate an entire year to a monk-like focus of ethics. Quite a feat for one who'd invested years as an enthusiastic member of my older sister's pack, the top dog who had gleefully taught me to shoplift, smoke, and explore drugs. My commitment would require me to embrace abstinence from all my vices, which would include a vow to be completely honest in word as well as deed.

Not to suggest I was dishonest by nature. Lying was never a strong suit, and even when I was completely forthright, undeserved guilt shone from my eyes. Yet most of us find stark truth is not our default mechanism in daily life. Particularly those who are still floundering within the mire of teenage years. So—no lies. This translated to include: no evasion, no avoidance, no excuses.

It was a painful choice in many circumstances, one never easy, but oddly liberating. Of course, tact was out the window during my quest and I nearly got thrown in jail when my sister was 'holding' and a cop asked if anyone was carrying pot, yet I learned how much easier life is when you have nothing to hide. The quest was never fully abandoned by me, though I now incorporate tact and a measure of discretion. However, I could never be comfortable in life without my True North of living in truth. It keeps me accountable, even when I'd rather not face uncomfortable truths that force me to address my choices, make amends, and modify my behavior.

One of those choices took me decades to confront.

My heroes were selected by a damaged psyche.

I was irresistibly drawn to narcissists.

Along with my brother, and my high school boyfriend, the two girls my childhood self admired most fell into that category.

My sister was intelligent enough to skip grades, yet also clever enough to charm her way out of repercussions. She learned early on that her attractiveness could garner attention, and how enamored males could provide the means to avoid financial responsibility. As an eight-year-old kid, the older sister I worshiped taught and encouraged me to lie, to steal, to smoke, to ditch class, and even to experiment with various intoxicating substances. She'd go up to the open door at my gym class and wave me over, whispering, "I'm going to pull the fire alarm, be ready."

Denise had a gift for recklessness.

Yet with her incredible talents, sparkling intelligence, and histrionic personality how could I help but worship her? When she was eight, in the private school she attended before dad's untimely demise, one assignment had been to "describe your family." A short bio to introduce yourself and your roots. A little while later, the teacher called my mom. Apparently, the assignment didn't go as planned. Denise's handwritten story apparently described in vivid detail how she'd actually been abandoned by her real parents at birth and found in a trashcan. As it turned out, her real parents were royalty.

When she was fourteen or so, feeling wronged and misunderstood in a very dramatic way, she wrote a story about a wronged and misunderstood boy named David. Of course, the boy ran away as she so often threatened to do, then tragically died at the end. The conclusion was a poignant letter where the main character poured out his heart and metaphorically shook his finger at those who'd treated him poorly. The last words of that letter were also the title of her saga: "Love, David."

I read it, turning the pages as fast I could, the story was as good as any one of my favorite books. At the end, I wept.

She could aptly play piano, flute, and guitar. Sporting a lovely voice, she could sing sweetly and write astonishingly good songs, poems, and stories. Her pristine handwriting could be mistaken for professional calligraphy. A bundle of potential yet with little to no empathy, nor any concern for the results of her destruction.

In a heartbeat she could weave a tale sure to garner the sympathy of all. In high school, she even managed to persuade her best friend's family to foster her. That lasted (according to her recounting) until the first time her 'new' mother told her to do the dishes. According to my sister, she grabbed her LSD from the drawer, along with her clothes (stuffed into a duffel bag), took two hits and ran to the road with her thumb out, waiting for a ride.

Along with this initiation into the most destructive choices in life, Denise also pulled me into an exploration of metaphysics, which would initiate my lifelong quest of achieving self-awareness. We quickly mastered the basics of numerology, which proved a fascinating study.

She then introduced me to astrology, and lent me the books she bought but was too impatient to read more than once. Years later, she'd convince me to become a vegetarian, a lifestyle I faithfully (and happily) embraced for over two decades. Her charisma radiated, her talent bordered on genius and appeared limitless. Mine chugged slowly, faltered frequently, so she was the shooting star while I gazed upward in awe.

In 1981, an improvisational comedy team opened up at Golden West College. At our first show, along with our crazy antics and some truly skillful comedy bits by a very young Steve Odekirk (who'd go on to write the cult-classic, *Kung Pow: Enter the Fist*, along with co-writing spectacular comedies, including one of my favorites, *Bruce Almighty*), my secret and fervent desire was to perform a musical number. Peering back into my early years of hopeful stardom, I feel pangs of affection. I can still see me—long, straight hair and glasses, blue jean skirt and a peasant blouse, quaking inside while earnestly playing an old Peter, Paul, and Mary tune. Over a decade too late to be the hippie chick I somehow imagined myself to be. And then out strode my sister.

I'd persuaded the director to let my "super talented sister" perform a song. She did not disappoint. Finding a book of ancient poems translated from the original Greek in the college library, she'd selected one and added a catchy, infectious rhythm. She performed like an old-fashioned troubadour: no chair just her brilliant charisma and an acoustic guitar perched on one knee. You could feel the energy ripple out, touching the crowd, who responded like a crowd of flowers bending towards the sun. Soon she had the whole audience enthusiastically singing along with the chorus: "Music, music, it's my best friend."

The song was such a delightful tune, who could resist? The applause was thunderous.

I idolized her.

My second role model appeared when I was fourteen.

Two years older, with a keen intelligence and quick wits, also able to nimbly play guitar and sing, she too seemed like a goddess. Every man that met Sally appeared to fall madly in love, and in my naivety it made total sense. She was so brilliant and charming and talented, of course they adored her!

For a child whose shameful secret was that she was not worthy of love, this appeared to be a superpower.

Decades later, I would read of a scientific experiment where complete strangers would be brought together, instructed to hold hands and gaze steadily into each other's eyes. Most of the participants reported distinctly feeling as if they were 'falling in love.'

Prolonged eye contact has been thought to trigger a release of phenethylamine and oxytocin, chemicals that appear to be responsible for feelings of attraction. Phenylethylamine produces the neurochemical dopamine, and contributes to the pleasurable, over-the-world feeling experienced with deep attraction. Oxytocin, often dubbed the 'love chemical,' is similarly linked to long-term bonding and intense feelings of commitment.

In two studies, subjects induced to exchange a mutual unbroken gaze for 2 min with a stranger of the opposite sex reported increased feelings of passionate love for each other. In Study I, 96 subjects were run in the four combinations of gazing at the other's hands or eyes, or in a fifth condition in which the subject was asked to count the other's eye blinks. Subjects who were gazing at their partner's eyes, and whose partner was gazing back reported significantly higher feelings of affection than subjects in any other condition. They also reported greater liking than all subjects except those in the eye blink counting condition. In Study II, with 72 subjects, those who engaged in mutual gaze increased significantly their feelings of passionate love, dispositional love, and liking for their partner. This effect occurred only for subjects who were identified on a separate task as more likely to rely on cues from their own behavior in defining their attributes. —Journal of Research in Personality, Volume 23, Issue 2, June 1989, Pages 145-161

Once I asked her how she could make every man we knew fall in love with her, and she said, "I guess I just know how to listen." Yet as the years crept by, I began to notice how she'd set it up and pretty much cultivate her target. She was very good at gazing into your eyes without looking away or even blinking, encouraging people to share their fears, their hopes...their secrets. I'd watch her squeezing their emotional biceps, practically cooing, "My what a big strong caretaker you are!"

Unfortunately, while falling in love was a favorite hobby, staying in love was altogether different. Her pattern became clear. Find a guy, enjoy the "in love" stage, then cultivate their ability to be a caretaker. Then she'd shift into "Please take care of me," mode, manipulating them into pretty much doing everything, until she got bored. If the desired dissolution of the relationship wasn't easy to arrange she'd edge towards meanness, often accompanied by drinking, as she maneuvered into the break-up. Curiously, she developed a fascinating ability. Instead of the usual dramatic fights that most folks utilize to end a relationship, she often manipulated the situation so her partners would calmly agree to a break-up. This way they could still be friends, there was no blame, and if the need arose, they would still be willing to provide whatever assistance she desired.

She was generous with her cast-offs. One fellow became my first serious (and truly mature) boyfriend. When my curiosity got the better of me, I finally worked up the nerve to ask him why they broke up. He laughed and told me that Sally was never serious about love, that she was always just shopping. What on earth did that mean?

"She said to me, let's discuss how we're going to handle it when we break up."

This apparently threw him completely. Robert was a sincere, sweet man who *wanted* to fall in love. Hearing her speak so dispassionately about the inevitability of their break-up caught him by surprise. It also told him more about the nature of her emotions than perhaps she realized. He'd majored in psychology and he perceived a calculation there that was very revealing.

His response was simply, "Why wait?"

They broke up but remained friends. Yet he perceived what would elude me for decades to come, even though she could hurt me with the same indifference I'd seen her display with others. Boldly approaching my now boyfriend Rob to rub his shoulders, leaning in to say softly, *"Someone's woman has been neglecting him."* Not even caring if I overheard. As I had been conditioned to do by my childhood of neglect, I buried my feelings and blamed myself.

One vivid story sticks out from my youth. A harmless tale that speaks volumes about what I wanted to hear, and how that colored my perspective. My decision to believe what I wanted to believe, despite evidence to the contrary.

I was about sixteen. Intellectually, on top of the world, poring through those pop psychology books and delving into metaphysical explorations. Emotionally though, I was not yet able to distinguish between actual care and a natural con. My friend Sally was coming to visit from another state. In anticipation, I scraped together enough cash to purchase a Marie Callendar's deep dish apple pie. Being raised in a home with few cooked meals, this frozen dessert was the ultimate in luxury to me. I baked it fresh and offered a juicy piece à la mode to my friend, accompanied by a fragrant mug of hot chocolate made from those handy packets.

I said, "Isn't this the most delicious pie?"

I was thrilled and secretly proud to present such a tasty dessert.

She looked at me with astonished pity and said, "Have you never eaten a *real* pie?"

Humbled and now embarrassed for reasons that were unclear, I admitted my lack. She was a master at making me feel both validated and ashamed all at once.

Examining me with an expression of sympathy and regret, she dramatically announced, "I will make you a *real* pie and *real* hot chocolate."

It was as if she was bestowing upon me the riches of a kingdom I'd faintly heard about in a distant land, or perhaps in a TV sitcom far, far away.

Naturally, I was filled with gratitude, practically choked up with emotion. So grateful to this girl who had neatly pointed out how lacking my life was, how insignificant (and clearly awful) my attempt to provide a treat was, and how *she would rescue me* from my pitifully limited world. Even better, *she* would cook for me! Provide an experience of mothering and nurturing my life clearly lacked, and offer it all up on a platter with gentle compassionate care. It's no wonder that my gratitude rivaled ecstasy. I felt so loved and cherished.

One small problem.

The promised reward never appeared.

Yup, as can often happen, she generously promised and it was the fantasy of being special that was meant to sustain me. I accepted this grand vow and responded *as if it were an action*, which it wasn't. Of course. Words are not actions.

Other similar promises were made, and when I was foolish enough to bring them up, the response was unexpected.

See, I have always felt truly grateful to be of service to people. Being able to do favors for others felt uncommonly good to me. Her reaction surprised and once again, shamed me. Sally would appear so over-burdened, so put out, making it starkly clear that her offer—this spontaneous grand gesture—was now an imposition, an onerous task and I should feel guilty, and then obligated to ease *her* pain.

Bizarre. Crazy. Uncomfortable.

The games a narcissist plays can twist your mind, for it's all about appearance. They have an instinct about whom to target, those hearts that endured neglect or abuse, the souls yearning to feel special, appreciated, and loved. They train you to be good pets, content with the occasional treat, so that you will wait patiently for their attention, which will be abruptly withdrawn if you dare to challenge their authority.

Despite what I now know, the truth is that I adored both women. There were endless days and nights of hilarity and fun.

I was a lonely girl and even if they had their own hidden agendas, their love and attention made me feel special. It felt like an honor to worship them, and our relationships only began to break down when my psyche healed enough that I could move into a state of accountability, a land where they did not wish to reside. Our relationships were also based on a particular power structure: we were *not* equals. When I grew into a space of feeling on the same level, there arose a need to put me back into my place.

Yet it runs deeper than that.

When love is based on imbalance, it's not real. Projecting our hopes of visibility, our yearning to be special onto the shoulders of one who seems larger than life isn't fair to either party. My fractured psyche sought out idols and they fit the role. When I healed, the very qualities that drew us together now pushed us apart.

They appeared to me like goddesses, simply because my invisibility, my diminished sense of self sought egos big enough to compensate for my lacks. Yet when I slipped off my leash, I then had to examine my heroes with a more realistic eye. My realizations shocked and dismayed me.

A curious thing had happened with those childhood idols, the ones who were so comfortable with lying and manipulating and casual destruction. It seemed as if they lost a part of their selves in the course of things. They continued on their paths of havoc and manipulation, but much more quietly.

My sister went on a spiritual bent. Starting with transcendental meditation, joining a spiritual family in Portland, then becoming a Moonie (a cult run by Reverend Moon), a week as a Scientologist, then onto a path of Eastern spirituality: Sant Mat. The last, she informed me loftily, is The Path of the Saints. Clearly nothing but the most exclusive spiritual path would do. Apparently, anyone with whom she would interact would themselves become a saint within four lives. She could generously bestow this spiritual gift simply by being in our presence.

When she needed a place to stay, my first husband and I innocently welcomed her into our home. The sister I worshipped could do no wrong in my eyes.

A toxic narcissist is a fascinating case study. They love to wreak havoc, to toss a metaphorical bomb into a room and see what blows up. When she stayed with me, she'd cozy up, persuading me to confide any unhappiness, then did the same with my husband. The fireworks began when she shared the confided complaints and set us both to fighting.

Many I've known have gone through similar struggles with narcissistic friends and family members. The games can seem so obvious in retrospect, but as we struggle with our fervent desire to do the right thing, the pain of working with those caught up in their own psychological patterns may be more than we can bear.

In her later years, Denise appeared content, still living off of the kindness of strangers, and for decades following a self-proclaimed guru who bestowed her brand of wisdom on those with enough money to pay for the privilege of enlightenment. A metaphysical center by all appearances that encourages a cult-like mentality.

Back in '86, this same guru promised her followers they would all be "lords of their own planet." Even then I couldn't see it. Denise's long-term goal had been based on the competitiveness of her youth. My sister... so incredibly talented and intelligent, and yet her ambition was not to be the best human she could be. What she craved was not enlightenment but power. She wanted to be a god.

Towards the end of her life, she did at last find peace. She stepped away from the slavish devotion to her guru and returned to her Vedic roots, the path that began with transcendental meditation. She focused on being a devotee, with a monk-like focus. Her profile on social media centered on love and spiritual devotion.

Yet I recognize my own ambivalence to her mystical persona as her focus depended on enforced positivity, which required an absolute acceptance with no confrontation or disagreement allowed. It felt dishonest, this need for me to stay silent or pretend to agree with her belief system, and worse, to ignore the impact of her choices. I was baffled. How could she skirt past any responsibility? How could she feel spiritually evolved while still dodging accountability?

Fascinating, really. In time I recognized a startling revelation. The ability of those damaged heroes to lie effortlessly to others, assisted them in lying, just as effortlessly, to themselves. My quest at age seventeen was an early attempt to reprogram myself, to break out of the pack. Yet to step away from the group dynamic is always risky and painful.

Avoiding responsibility for choices became the default mechanism for survival within my pack. This required a nearly constant focus on blaming outside circumstances, or pointing fingers at others, automatically shifting blame for any unpleasant reality their choices created. Some of those choices led to unbelievable chaos or tragedy, the memories of which still makes me wince. Mostly because for years I was culpable.

I'd avert eyes to their choices and instead of confrontation, attempt to "unconditionally love" them. In part, admittedly, because I let myself be manipulated as well. The alpha dogs didn't want to be challenged for any of their choices, and they used me to provide cover. I had to force myself to recognize how they'd hurt and use people I truly cared for, how newly acquired friends trusted my best friend because I vouched for her, and my friends trusted *me*. There's a devastating realization, agonizing to admit. To realize with horror and chagrin, how my unspoken endorsement engendered complete trust, which resulted in mayhem.

However—and here's the thing—destruction and chaos was not their conscious intention. In fact, from their perspective it is *they* who are the victims here. That may be what destroyed the last person. He couldn't take the pressure of the role my former friend had thrust upon him. She'd taken in yet another wounded soul, one with crippling insecurity and painful social anxiety. Building up his ego with her emotional massage until he too was hopelessly enamored and unable to perceive the leash she quietly attached, then yanking on that chain until he exploded with the panicked rage of an abandoned pet turned feral.

The story of how he was now a monster, a victimizer, and she, the helpless, ever-suffering damsel felt painfully familiar. I recognize with regret and deep pain, how she has become so 'disguised to herself' she can't perceive her actions any more clearly than others can.

Those we may perceive as monsters are simply caught up in their own psychological patterns. We unwittingly stumble onto a game board and become part of the game. Narcissists are especially skilled at turning us into game pieces, training us to enable their destructive behavior. My pattern of neglect and abuse was a perfect fit. Without the awareness of these patterns, we can all stagger right into the danger zone.

Beware of the Narcissist.

What good is that hand-lettered sign if we are not yet able to perceive it?

For years, I patted myself on the back for my self-awareness, my commitment to self-honesty. If someone were to call me out on something, chances are pretty darn good that I'm well aware of that failing and have already beat myself up more times than I can count. Those insecurities, faults, mistakes, and shameful admissions were lodged in my soul and all too frequently reviewed. Nudge me and the door would be kicked open and all my secrets would tumble out.

One failing pointedly eluded my scrutiny.

This was my inability to perceive hurtful people honestly. When those I adored acted out, whether against others, or me I'd either completely ignore it or bite my lip in order to remain loyal. My desperate need to be loved meant I'd tolerate meanness, cruel words, hurtful actions. I'd make excuses for their choices, insist they were good people at heart, that they didn't know better.

Why? As a child, I never experienced the unconditional love every child craves. The nurturing, the comfort, the acceptance, and the love were starkly absent from my life. Perhaps I didn't consciously recognize this was somehow wrong, but subconsciously I certainly knew and recognized this lack as a failing. My clever sister was quick enough to pick up on that and use my own integrity against me. The secret fear was not so secret to her and she never hesitated to let me know.

If I didn't love her unconditionally, I was a monster.

Starting with Robert, every close friend could perceive my former friend and both siblings with clear eyes. No matter my excuses or attempts to somehow paint a prettier picture, they could see what I refused to look at. In the end, one can't blame people for their natures, we must take responsibility for our own choices.

There's an old parable heard long ago that really had an impact.

Scorpion needs to cross a river but has no means. He scuttles up and down the mossy bank trying to figure out a solution. He spots a frog hopping about on the many rocks dotting the river. The answer is obvious now.

Scorpion calls out, "Frog, I need to cross the river, please carry me on your back!"

The frog hops closer and responds, "No. If I do that you'll sting me."

"I promise not to sting you," Scorpion says.

"I don't believe you. Your sting is deadly and I can't take that chance."

"Why would I do that after you helped me? If I were to sting you while in the river, we'd both drown! I simply need to cross and then I'll crawl off and go my own way," says Scorpion persuasively. He continues on to make his case, doing his best to convince the frog to assist him. Finally Frog relents.

He edges close enough to the riverbank to allow the scorpion to scramble onto his back. Carefully, he hops from stone to stone, maneuvering his way across the river. About halfway across, the scorpion sinks his poisonous tail into the frog's back.

Shocked, Frog screams. "Why did you sting me after all your promises? Now we are both doomed."

Scorpion shrugs and responds, "It's my nature."

This potent fable came to me when I was in my late twenties. I could feel the clarity this truth prompted reverberating through my soul in regard to my beautiful, talented sister and charismatic friend. Yet what could I do? Guilt and obligation still had me in its fearsome grip.

Their destructive choices were part of their nature. The urge to take advantage of the trust of others was also part of their nature.

My nature was to trust.

No matter how many excuses I could make, there is no denying my responsibility. I introduced too many frogs to the scorpions in my life. It would take courage, it would require me to acknowledge my own shameful acts of enabling, in order to move forward into a more constructive choice. The chains that held me would need to be broken by my own awareness.

As a child, I didn't believe in my own invisible self because I had yet to develop a viable personality. So instead, I believed in the selves of others even when their destructive acts became too obvious to ignore.

There have been many invaluable lessons in my life.

The most important one remains: *Be true to yourself and be honest with yourself, even when (especially when) it's too painful to admit.*

It's the only way we survive with awareness intact. When we lie to others, they'll eventually discover the truth, and when they do, they'll walk away without a moment's hesitation. When we lie to ourselves, who is it that turns away and where does she go?

Being true to yourself is only possible when we dig deeply enough to discover who we are. If we feel a diminished sense of self, we seek out others whose masks we then adopt as our own. When that occurs we become invested in protecting those we relied upon to provide us with a shelter for our lonely souls. We chain ourselves to their patterns which now become our own. Our fear keeps us enslaved and no matter how many signs are pounded into the ground, we'll ignore them as we continue to be drawn to personalities with familiar patterns. That is until we choose to consciously slip off the collar and finally walk free.

It is every person's destiny to discover and then become her truest self. Even if that means we must then stride vigorously away from the familiar pack, and find our own way home.

SUGGESTED FOCUS:

Time to reflect on past choices involving others that may still make you wince. If faced with a similar situation today, could you make a more constructive choice? If so, then comfort yourself with the realization that the lesson has been learned. Now it's time to forgive yourself for any decisions that still haunt you. Trust you can make better choices as long as you're willing to face your truth.

AFFIRMATION: <u>I am always doing the best I can in every circumstance. When I know better, I do better. I support my growth without judgment.</u>

REVIEW:

Write down a list of your most uncomfortable choices in regard to others. Anytime you chose to 'go along with the crowd' with an action that you now regret. Those times you didn't speak up but knew you should. The moment points when you were afraid to confront or say, "No," only to face the pain of a destructive outcome.

Now is when we must once again take on the mantle of the Oversoul. Now you are the future self that knows better. This exercise is two-fold.

The first one requires us to be brave enough to forgive ourselves for any action or choice that hurt another, and to forgive ourselves for our inaction as well. Write a letter from the You of now, who is the 'future self' to the younger You. Offer up support and encouragement, forgiveness and compassion. Let your own love wash over the painful scars of your past choices. We cannot forgive anyone until we learn how to forgive ourselves.

*The second exercise is one that is now familiar. We are going to take those past moments and create alternate endings. It's important to let yourself **feel** the positive emotions in these restructured past events. Picture yourself making different* *choices and righting past wrongs. Remember, within our quantum universe, every probability plays out. You can add strength and a healing energy that is potent enough to not only powerfully and positively affect your emotional wellbeing, the energy can ripple out and impact the probabilities of those with whom you interacted.*

PART THREE

SELF-TRANSFORMATION: WHO MIGHT I BECOME?

FOURTEEN
LIFE SCULPTORS

We're all life-sculptors.
Chipping away erroneous
bits
of concrete memories,
tracing the vision of
inner eyes.
Releasing fragmented symbols
trapped within
rocky beliefs
or slick judgments held
suspended
in a moment of doubt.

Dreaming of a
Perfect Self,
pristine and unsullied
by time's wagging finger.
Until the cracks in
the marble
reveal the truth
we've hidden
in plain sight.

FIFTEEN
PUTTING MY PAST IN FRONT OF ME

I have realized that the past and future are real illusion, that they exist in the present, which is what there is and all there is.

ALAN WATTS

The physical framework appears to our eyes as a fixed reality. What we see is what we get.

As giggling children, we are infinitely more playful. We can envision a world where a dashing Peter Pan takes to the sky and a courageous young Dorothy teams up with a talking Scarecrow and tenderhearted Tin Woodman. We easily dream of magical companions and happily imagine our silly stuffed Pooh-bear skitters about and giggles along with us.

When we transition to become adults, we are sternly reminded to put aside those seemingly childish notions. We are told to embrace the hard, cold reality that is the crux of being a sensible grownup. No matter what we intuitively grasped as children, we may grow convinced over the years there is only one fixed reality, that our adventurous, fanciful dreams are unreal, and the past is immutable.

Because of this indoctrination, it can be easy to forget the natural fluidity of creation. Our imaginative arteries may harden, which can severely restrict the flow of our thoughts in order to conform to the limiting beliefs we feel forced to adopt. It can happen to all of us, depending on the circumstance.

The casual programming is all around us, there are stereotypes of aging, for example, that we automatically absorb. We may be told we'll grow frail, yet there are stunning examples of women in their 50's, 60's, 70's, 80's and beyond who are in peak physical condition. One example is Sister Madonna Buder, nicknamed The Iron Nun. By age 86, this remarkable woman completed over 360 triathlons and 45 Ironmans, the latter being a three-part race consisting of a 2.4 mile swim, a 112-mile bike ride and a full marathon.

If we buy into the programming of unproductive yet pervasive myths, we may forget that every creation, every action, every choice begins within our imagination. Every circumstance we encounter originates from a belief as changeable as our wardrobe. Because of an unconscious adaption to earlier encounters, we may have tucked ourselves into confining beliefs like a businessman from the 1940s slipping into a classic suit and designer tie. The suit and tie beautifully fit the beliefs being explored at the time, beliefs from a distant childhood or even from other experiences in a far removed life when we peered out of different eyes. We forgot there are other outfits, or if we do remember, it's more with a wistful longing of what we could wear *if only...*

What we must remember is that our greatest tool in reality creation is a flexible imagination. What I mean by this is not the limited idea we've been taught. We must discard the cramped notion of imagination being nothing more than a rejuvenating escape from the humdrum routine of daily life.

Every reality we encounter begins within our imagination.

Every dazzling invention, every unique innovation, every startling change begins with the inkling of an idea. At first the spark of a concept may seem farfetched and fanciful. Like a strange fruit we've never tried, we tentatively nibble at it, wondering if it suits our taste or not.

Every unifying relationship, every baffling circumstance, every delicious reality we encounter begins as a flicker of light within our imagination. Which means, whether we like it or not, we *imagined* ourselves into the dastardly circumstances we abhor, as fervently as we imagined ourselves into delightful situations we adore.

Here's an intriguing tidbit.

Experiments have suggested that people with falsely implanted memories will build on those memories even to the point of creating solid identities based on events that never actually occurred.

A distinguished Professor at the University of California, Irvine, Elizabeth Loftus has been at the forefront of psychological research into the intense controversy of repressed memories. She took her exploration further by delving into groundbreaking research exploring the possibility of implanting false memories. The experiment was first created by an undergraduate student of Professor Loftus, Jim Coan. The study methodology was later refined for his senior thesis, in collaboration with his professor, and graduate student, Jacqueline Pickrell.

In 1995 they initiated a provocative study. Could a person be convinced that a fictitious occurrence was actually real? So real that they would then actively recall equally fictitious details on their own?

They recruited 24 participants then set the stage, contacting relatives of each participant, requesting information about three childhood events. The required situations would need to have occurred between the ages of four and six years old, be fairly easy to recall, and free of trauma or pain. Here's where it gets interesting. With the intention of creating a false memory, the researchers would also include an event that didn't actually happen. The setting for each participant would be the same—a supposed memory of getting lost in a shopping mall. To establish plausibility, families were asked to help flesh out the particulars by providing enough details of an actual mall where the child might have wandered.

Each member participating was informed that the study involved recollection of childhood memories and their ability to pull up specific details. The subjects all received notes of the four events (the three that actually occurred along with the fictional scenario) and were instructed to jot down which ones they could recall, providing as many details as possible.

There was a follow-up interview after a week where they were prompted to remember the incidents, and encouraged to provide further details. A second interview was conducted after another week had passed. The idea being that the interlude between interviews would allow the participants to consider and review the childhood events. In each follow-up, those involved in the study were successfully able to deepen their recall and pull up more extensive details.

The experiment successfully persuaded the participants to actively recall memories in an event that hadn't actually occurred, and when the study concluded, they were informed one of the recalled events was false, but which one? When asked to differentiate between the true and false occurrence, five of the twenty-four believed firmly that the 'lost in the mall' event was the real deal. This prompted further research as methods were refined, and the results expanded and became even more telling. Later studies by other researchers found false memories could successfully be implanted in up to forty to fifty percent of participants.

During the course of the initial experiment and others, the participants did not recall the false memory at first but were able to after being encouraged to do so over a period of weeks. The more they provided details and then were prompted to 'remember' those details, the easier it became. Those memories not only were fleshed out, they became imbued with emotion.

Every memory becomes more real and feels more authentic with every repeated viewing. We may feel the loss of love with keen bitterness or sharp regret. A traumatic event remembered can still trigger panic attacks and physiological response. Recalling a situation that incurred anger can set our heart pounding as our blood pressure elevates.

When we peer back and remember a casual or seminal moment—a festive birthday party, a vacation where we walked barefoot on hot sands and dove into cool waves, a holiday where our fondest wishes were fulfilled or our hopes were crushed and we cried ourselves to sleep—each of those memories is suffused with feeling. Those emotions add vivid color and astonishing depth to the memories, which then become a part of our personal mythology. Even the memories of favorite books, shows, films, or an evocative tune will stir our emotions and prompt a feeling-tone within our imaginative selves.

Ever have a dream so real that you're not actually certain whether it really was a dream? Our nocturnal adventures are intrinsically linked to our imaginative prowess, and inventors, musicians, artists, and storytellers alike have all shared fascinating tales of how dreams inspired phenomenal creations.

Our sleeping dreams may arise from an unconscious use of imagination but within our daydreams we are active participants. Many success stories regularly share how focused visualization resulted in beating the odds.

Oprah Winfrey watched her grandmother struggle and began telling herself regularly, "My life won't be like this. My life won't be like this, it will be better." She continued to use this phrase as a focus as her level of success rose. Her recognition of how concentrating on this affirmation, and believing it to be absolutely true, changed her life and has prompted her to repeatedly encourage visualization and positive thinking as a means to accomplishment.

Just as we may pull up past memories to reinforce a belief formed out of past events that holidays are awful or beach vacations soothe the soul, visualizations create future 'memories' that provide a foundation for our beliefs. Oprah's affirmation utilized the same method explored in the experiment of false memory by deliberately creating a *future* memory. The more she focused on this 'memory,' the more real it became.

She might have used her past instead as proof she couldn't succeed. Focusing on the memory of her grandmother's struggle, she might have said, "Life is hard and I'm stuck in this role forever." The unpleasant memory then would become a core belief, which would guide her to unconsciously choose situations to fulfill her expectation of struggle and unhappiness.

Oprah made a different choice and chose to believe in a different future.

Volleyball teammates, Kerri Walsh and Misty May-Treanor are Gold Medal winners who credit meditation and visualization for their success. Another Gold Medalist, Lindsey Vonn, one of the top female skiers in history, shared how her mental practice of visualization consistently provides a competitive edge on the course.

Jim Carrey was a typical struggling-to-succeed actor who utilized visualization in a unique way. He wrote out a check to himself for ten millions dollars and would keep that in his back pocket, handily accessible to pull out so he could concentrate and visualize. The paycheck for his role in the movie, *Dumb and Dumber,* exactly matched his focus. He consistently credits visualization for his phenomenal success.

Every pristine moment, every casual breath begins within the imagination. Any change we create, whether minuscule or momentous, is birthed within our imagination. We don't always remember this, and much of our planning will be accomplished within nocturnal adventures, casual daydreams, or other aspects of our unconscious.

In this sense, every single day is a dream that first begins within the creative power of our mind's eye. Yet there is another tool available within our imagination that combines the power of visualization with the awareness of how influential our memories can be.

One of my most useful and evocative exercises has been to create alternate pasts. To infuse alternate backgrounds with as much fervent emotion and true passion as I can muster. Because my acceptance of the fluidity of the nature of reality allows me greater freedom in this regard, I can easily tell myself quite firmly how this 'imagined' past is now a legitimate alternate history.

Yesterday is just a memory, after all.

Those memories, chosen or 'actual,' are how we form our identities, our opinions of whom we might be, and even what we can accomplish. Recognizing this, we can utilize the incredible power of visualization to remind ourselves how this newly created past is just as valid and is indeed the one we firmly choose to remember. Just as we've practiced in earlier exercises.

This practice, suggested within *The Nature of Personal Reality by Jane Roberts,* began as a handy therapeutic tool that I successfully utilized to break an annoying, destructive habit of reinforcing unwanted beliefs and an equally unappealing self-image, by dredging up 'proof' from my past. There were many beliefs that plagued me as a child and a teen, ranging from feeling as hideous as the lead character in *The Elephant Man* to being convinced I was a bad person unworthy of love.

I still remember as a child cringing if someone looked my way, then glaring back defiantly, certain their stares were based on a revulsion they dared not vocalize. There was no need for me to consciously remind myself, for our beliefs are woven into the fabric of our souls. My mom's oft-repeated phrase of wishing her children had died instead of our father was proof enough that I was unworthy of love.

In tenth grade, my friend Tana introduced me to Brian, the bright and shiny narcissist who would become my first boyfriend. My fractured psyche and deflated ego was drawn to him like a moth to a destructive flame. Over the course of the year, I would fall madly, hopelessly in love, or so I thought. My mom was in college, simultaneously working at my Aunt's restaurant four nights a week. At an age where I could no longer endure the burning pinch of loneliness in the ever-empty apartment, I felt like an abandoned pet, desperate to find a home. When Brian and his brother moved from their dad's place in Tustin, California to live with their mother in faraway Altadena, leaving the high school we shared, my life shattered. My loneliness was agonizing. The only solution I could imagine was to drop out of school, and sneakily move in with him, hiding in the converted garage that had become his bedroom.

There were no objections from my mom who barely seemed to notice I'd gone. Previously, whenever my reflections took me back to examine this past, the regrets I felt regarding my life choices nearly choked me. The lack of stability I experienced was compounded by a complete inability to grasp the impact those choices might have on my future. Without a responsible caregiver around to help me perceive the point in education or even goals, I threw away possibilities that I didn't even know existed.

My self-education was productive, yet lacking. My thirst for knowledge led me to study history, philosophy, psychology, metaphysics, and even various religions. Yet I knew nothing of the mechanics of algebra nor the giddy pleasures of a high school prom. When I peered back regretfully at my past—the chaos, the destructive choices, the careless tossing away of potential life experiences—the losses staggered me. My humiliation over my unrecognized foolishness rivaled the secret shame of being an unwanted child.

There was more proof of my ability to fail than there was hope I could succeed at anything.

This needed to change.

My first attempt took place over a weekend. Spare time was usually dedicated to reading fiction or voraciously studying whatever new topic had caught my attention. Over the period of three days, I instead constructed a new history for me, starting at age three. I gave myself free rein, allowing the story to be written without any restrictions.

Instead of meeting my abusive soon-to-be stepfather Ray, I imagined instead that my mom became involved with a kind and stable fellow with a daughter my age. *He* played piano and encouraged my mom to go back to school. *His* sister (my new aunt) was a writer who became close to my mom. And on and on and on... This was my personal story, my alternate history, and within it I could paint any picture that brought satisfaction and healing. I infused this story with emotion and pleasure. It became a meditative journey as my imaginative self traced a new life history. All the choices I'd made in my current history could be redrawn. This alternate self not only began to take on emotional life for me, *she* provided a healing that took me by surprise.

Just as I'd vicariously peeked through the eyes of fictional heroes like Dorothy in the *Wonderful Wizard of Oz*, just as I imaginatively waved a magical wand like Harry Potter, I became immersed within the imaginary pages of my alternate history.

The result?

A feeling of euphoria and relief washed over me and lingered for well over a week. Even better, I felt stronger, more capable, more certain than I'd ever experienced.

Quantum mechanics spawned a theory of a multiverse, often referred to as the Many Worlds theory. This supposes that every possibility that can occur does occur. Just as we could twirl the dial of a radio to select a favorite station, we tune into a specific probability and call it reality. Yet other versions of us adjust the frequency, tuning into alternate probabilities and then distinguishing what they experience as reality as well. One 'me' decides to go left to avoid traffic, and the other chooses to go right and is late to her appointment. There is a version of me who chose to play guitar and a version who chose to learn the bass given to my sister when I was ten.

What is fascinating to consider is that if we incorporate the idea of Jung's collective unconscious, which suggests that along with our singular mental focus there is a vast pool of energy where all ideas, thoughts, and dreams are shared, we can tune directly into every single probable self that could (and therefore according to this theory *does*) exist.

When we focus on what we call a definitive memory based on actual events, we form a probable identity that we then fold into our collective idea of Who I Am.

I am... the eight-year old that felt unloved.

I am... the fourteen year old who chose a boy who would

treat me poorly and reinforce my belief that I didn't deserve to be loved.

If I suddenly developed amnesia, neither one of those memories would be active, and my identity would then be based on whatever memories were shared with me. Since I don't have amnesia, my current identity is based instead on whatever memories I unconsciously *or* deliberately select as a primary focus.

If a parent tells us we were exceptionally clever children and (like the experiment with false memory) provides details and proof, we absorb this information and incorporate it into our idea of whom we might be. Likewise if we were told that we were clumsy and awkward, we could unconsciously cling to that image and remind ourselves frequently that we need to be careful because we've always been uncoordinated.

My concept of myself is based on who I believe I am.

When I devoted a weekend to carefully constructing a detailed alternate probability, the exercise provided a foundation for an alternate version of myself.

My present moment now had a different backstory to provide a setting for a new plot line. If I am a product of my past, and I create an alternate history, I change my future. Just as Oprah created an alternate future for her childhood self to grow towards, I created an alternate past for my present self from which I could draw emotional sustenance.

Some may see this as merely a useful tool for altering one's current perspective, as it absolutely will do. Some may take it a step further and consider the possibility these probable pasts have as much validity within a quantum universe as the one physically experienced.

In the moment point I'm experiencing, I recognize a fluidity allowing me to create my past as surely as I create my future. What future do you wish to create? It's time to choose. Let's build a yesterday that creates an enticing and supportive tomorrow.

SUGGESTED FOCUS:

We've explored and experimented with the idea of a probable past. Let's take that a step further. Pick an age or a significant turning point in your past. Now, from that point, turn a corner. For my exploration, I have chosen various time periods. Age six, age ten, age twelve, age seventeen, and so on. Select one and create a completely new life based from that starting point. Let your imagination flow. This is your story and you call the shots. Follow it through as best you can to your current moment. Flesh out the details. Create the people you met, the paths you explored.

Most importantly, feel the emotions of your new probable past. Feel the successes, the triumphs, and the love. Don't hold yourself back by so-called logic. This probable life within the imagination is yours to create. The emotional satisfaction will be just as fulfilling as any "real" events from your experienced past. Even better, that alternate reality, that vivid and emotionally sustaining probability now exists within a quantum universe. You brought Her to life! Now her talents, achievements, wins, strength, insight, knowledge and experience, are available for you to draw upon. His or Her experience is also yours.

AFFIRMATION: I am nourished, strengthened, invigorated, and supported by all aspects of my Being. I open myself up to my bank of probable selves and all of their experiences enrich my life.

REVIEW:

Write a diary excerpt from the perspective of one of your probable past selves. You can do this at any age, or even several various ages where you have set up probable past histories. Explore 'her' emotions. Now take it a step further and from 'her or his' perspective write down future goals and dreams. Who did 'she' imagine herself becoming? What goals did 'he' yearn to accomplish?

How can 'she' enrich your current experience? Visualize the chosen probabilities as probable selves who can advise and encourage you at any point. If you face any particular challenges, how would 'he' handle the situation? Write down 'her' perspective and explore new options.

SIXTEEN
EMBRACING THE DISCOMFORT ZONE

People have a hard time letting go of their suffering. Out of a fear of the unknown, they prefer suffering that is familiar.

THÍCH NHẤT HẠNH

Many years ago, I gravitated towards a book by Gloria Steinem called "Revolution From Within." She shared a realization about her own childhood-based comfort zone, and how this comfort zone relied on a familiarity of being drenched in misery, with bouts of nail-biting anxiety and bitter strife.

Having been raised similarly in an unnerving environment of nearly constant crisis, I experienced a jolt of recognition. Clearly my comfort zone needed to be drastically revamped too. Yet this would require me to deliberately *choose* to step out of a dynamic as comfortable and familiar as those shabby only-to-be-worn-at-home sweat-pants. We touched on this in Chapter Ten.

Initially, making such a radical change can trigger fears,

leave us as jittery as a caffeine addict in serious withdrawal. We have to catch ourselves in the act. The unconscious yearning for struggle means our brains are wired to automatically seek out drama and intense conflict. Something *feels* missing when we're no longer valiantly strapping on a broadsword to do battle with fierce dragons. Yet the only way to break the habit is to catch ourselves in the act and consciously, deliberately, choose to disengage from the addictive habit.

For me, this task was only made possible by developing a taste and an appetite for a quieter home life.

In comparison to my dramatic, anxiety-driven past, my current theme might seem rather boring to others. I no longer thrive on the crisis-fueled adrenalin rocketing through my fearful childhood, nor do I seek out the dramatic risks a victim-oriented focus can provide.

Instead, my pleasure may be simply a quiet satisfaction when a kind gesture encourages a smile. There's always the delicious exuberance of rocking my electric guitar, feeling the music take wing on a Saturday night or the exquisite release of a hearty laugh. I cherish the breathtaking pleasure of love with my wonderful friends and soul-family.

Yet for many of us, and certainly for me, such a change of focus requires steady practice and determined effort. Until we've rewired our brain, we'll find ourselves curving towards the pattern we're accustomed to following.

We've stepped out of the comfort zone into the *discomfort zone*.

The steps we take to initiate change are straightforward.

First we examine our current psychological dynamic. For those who've experienced abuse, strife, anxiety, or fearsome challenges in the earliest years, the question is: *Have I recreated that dynamic in my current life?*

What kind of friends, lovers, or coworkers are in my circle?

Usually the reason is straightforward: these people reflect the psychological dynamic that has become our comfort zone.

"I Want A Girl (Just Like The Girl That Married Dear Old Dad)," was a popular tune in 1911. The sentiment echoed a notion that appeared idyllic, to somehow encounter the same heartfelt love shared by our ever-so-happy parents. Yet for those whose childhood was instead fraught with neglect, abuse, or anxiety, the parental role models often represent a shadow aspect instead.

We do often "marry our parents" in that we are drawn to personalities who reflect a familiar dynamic. Similarly, we choose friends and even may find ourselves taking jobs where the supervisor or coworkers fit into that same box.

An absent or neglectful parent may instill within us a desperate need for validation or attention, yet there we are dating someone who ignores us or withdraws when we crave intimacy. Now we're once again trying to prove our worth to a substitute parent or finally gain the respect that was craved but never received in our childhood.

We may want to fervently believe that our current partner is nothing like an abusive caretaker, while carefully ignoring the biting criticism, stern expectations, or disapproving silence pointed our way. When we find ourselves having to justify or explain why we love someone who treats us poorly, the storyline is clearly locked into place.

Authority issues are a commonplace pattern for those raised by overbearing role models. Often this plays out in one of two scenarios. Either you're thrust into the role of authority figure, dealing with those who resist deadlines, or put off tasks, or act out—putting you in the position of being a nagging parent—or the reverse—feeling put upon and told what to do, and unable to grasp why this triggers such resistance and resentment inside.

What's so damn hard about carrying the coffee cup into the kitchen and putting it in the sink? Do I have to do everything around here?

I hate when my boss treats me like an irresponsible child, it wasn't my fault!

Next we have to honestly examine whether those choices are fulfilling us on some level, whether it be at the forefront, and obvious to our conscious mind, or deeply buried within our unconscious.

Do we feel satisfaction complaining about a stressful relationship or work situation? Do we feel victorious 'strapping on a sword and doing battle with the mythical dragon'?

If so, can we begin the process of stepping out of that dynamic?

Let's say there's a person at work that frustrates you. It could be a coworker who slacks off or complains incessantly. Perhaps it's a supervisor who treats you without respect.

Ask yourself, "Does this remind me of a situation from my childhood? Is there an echo there that I can pinpoint? Are there similar themes with my friends or lovers?"

If the answer is yes, there's some work to be done.

The first step is to remove the emotional pay-off.

Easier said than done.

What is the pay-off? Often times it's as simple as complaining about the situation.

The same aggravation from an earlier dynamic is reinforced by our focus, and then recreated endlessly.

So we must resist feeding the dynamic.

Venting serves a valuable purpose. Like a balloon being stretched beyond its capacity, without a good release of our emotions, we may feel ready to explode. It's so satisfying to let our bitter disappointment, our unexpressed anger, our nagging frustration tumble out; to release those bottled up feelings can be an intense relief.

There's a risk though, particularly for those of us with a childhood-based need for validation and attention.

It can feel a little too good.

The heartfelt sympathy, the comfort of compassion, the affirmation that we really were being treated poorly is an emotional pay-off that can be as deliciously satisfying as a sugar rush and just as addictive. Just like an energy slump, we may feel that emotional slump tugging at our self-esteem. Instead of a chocolate frosted donut with sprinkles and an energy drink, we tap into the emotions of a reoccurring situation that frustrates, angers, or otherwise enflames us. Just pulling up that scenario energizes us, the anger itself feels empowering!

Yet just like with that sugary snack, the initial buzz will be followed by another slump. We again crave that jolt of self-righteous indignation, *unconsciously programming ourselves to seek out situations that frustrate us* in order to provide the subsequent satisfaction of complaint.

The Emotional Payoff.

So what do we do?

Often it helps to write out our misery in a journal, or to share with a good friend, but how do we break the cycle of too much focus without veering into emotional repression?

For me, the answer has been a firm focus on accountability or what a friend called, "ownership."

It's a way of accepting that we got ourselves into this mess and *we have the power to change*, either changing ourselves or the outer circumstance.

We can and should take whatever action is possible. We are now in the process of identifying our patterns, taking ownership, and embracing our power to release or rewrite the dynamic to create a healthier, more viable and rewarding reality.

As we've explored in previous chapters, visualization is an immensely powerful tool recommended by many current spiritual teachers. We can utilize the power of our imagination to visualize a completely revamped scenario. For example, vividly imagine walking into work and being treated with respect. If something occurs to frustrate us, we can take a moment to close our eyes and once again, consciously imagine a scenario that brings us pleasure rather than aggravation. If it's too challenging to reframe the actual situation, substitute an alternate scene that provides an uplifting feeling of euphoria or fulfillment.

These are steps we can take to rewire the brain into expecting satisfaction and contentment within our daily life, rather than feeding the desire for sensation with memories fraught with aggravation or anxiety.

Next, we begin the process of identifying repeated patterns in our life, exploring our friendships and relationships, as well as scrutinizing past authority figures, parents along with supervisors and teachers, for similarities.

It's a beginning.

And a good one.

SUGGESTED FOCUS:

Just as an Olympic Gold Medal Winner visualizes the event repeatedly, focusing only on the win, so should we. Let's begin a practice of visualizing positive outcomes. Remember how every scenario plays out in some probability? The more energy we give to those alternate scenarios, the easier it becomes to make that the norm and draw that experience into our reality. Select a situation where you felt disappointed. Now vividly picture the same situation with your most satisfying outcome. Feel the emotion. Tell yourself, "<u>This probability is real. I release the need to complain because I have the power to change my life.</u>"

The more energy you invest in your mental and emotional focus, the easier it becomes to bring that picture to life.

. . .

AFFIRMATION: <u>I have the power to change my life. I focus on what I want and release what no longer brings value into my life.</u>

REVIEW:

The power of visualization is ours to utilize. Let's begin to practice with an area of our life where we yearn for change. The recommended length of time for this exercise is one month, and it only takes five minutes a day.

There may be many situations that require healing or transformation; let's pick one and begin. One example for me is when I moved to a new area and longed for nearby friends. I decided to apply the power of visualization to this goal. I'm happy to report that the outcome was favorable and I now have a solid circle of beautiful souls whom I truly cherish. This practice must go hand in hand with our accountability focus simply because we can't visualize something without also taking action.

One can't win a gold medal for skiing without getting on the slopes. Nor can we become a successful actor without being willing to study our lines. When we yearn for love, we must also be determined to perceive and break through our psychological patterns in order to facilitate a happy union. Which means that while doing this practice, it's vital to stay alert to any patterns that arise.

Picture it like shoveling snow out of a driveway so you can finally move forward. We take action by shoveling the snow but unless we keep inner eyes open, we may be heaving those shovelfuls of snow right back into our path. Which means it's mandatory that we give ourselves an encouraging nudge to pay close attention to any unconscious patterns that could hold us back.

To practice this method, choose an area where you feel most relaxed. The easiest choice is simply to sit in a comfortable chair with eyes closed. Inhale deeply through your nose and exhale through your mouth slowly and deeply until you feel yourself relax.

Focus on the area of life where you wish to see change. Is it a desire to feel strong and healthy? Then picture yourself striding with enthusiasm, bending easily, and flowing with health. Tell yourself, "I am strong and healthy, filled with energy and able to accomplish everything I desire with ease." (You can—and should—adjust the wording in whatever way feels right to you)

Repeat your chosen phrase while simultaneously visualizing yourself in an action or within an outcome that supports your vision. If you're working on a task, you can visualize yourself pumping a fist victoriously, or clinking glasses, or even jumping up and down. When I struggled with money issues, I visualized the words "PAID IN FULL" across each bill.

"This is my **true** reality. My former experience is now fading away as my true reality grows stronger. The truth is that I am strong and healthy, physically fit, and filled with energy."

Do this for five minutes and then let it go until the next day. If fears or doubt arise, simply acknowledge that the former reality had been in place for a while, pull up the visualization and remind yourself that your **true reality** is represented by your visualization.

Remember how Oprah repeated her phrase as she gazed at her grandmother? "My life won't be like this. My life won't be like this, it will be better."

"I am strong and healthy..."

This is also where we trust the universe to send us help.

Trust, action, accountability.

SEVENTEEN
PUSHING AGAINST A WALL

That which we persist in doing becomes easier to do, not that the nature of the thing has changed but that our power to do has increased.

RALPH WALDO EMERSON

For some reason, this quote reminds me of the adage: *The harder you push against a wall, the harder it pushes back.*

The wall is the perfect metaphor for a fixed belief. In retrospect it becomes obvious we can't make headway if we give up. Every challenge appears to magnify in proportion to our fear, until we reach a point where we are tempted to abandon our quest. The longer we gaze with minds-eye quivering in apprehension, the larger and more fearsome our problems seem to become. So instead of taking action, instead of persisting, we give up. The wall hasn't defeated us: we have defeated ourselves.

What really struck a chord within me about Emerson's

words is this: we can indeed continue to shove with fearful intensity against the wall, or we can choose to seek out cracks and crevices, insert nimble fingers, find footholds and heave ourselves over. Perhaps the wall doesn't extend as far as our eyes first perceive. A quick stroll to assess the situation might reveal that within a few footsteps there is an opening, allowing us to simply walk to the other side.

We can either perceive the wall as an insurmountable obstacle, feel powerless and give up, or flip our view into something new.

The irony here for most of us is this altered view may in the beginning be one of our greatest challenges. We've adapted to perceiving the wall as a massive, invincible, *permanent* obstruction, not realizing this is only our perception. It is our perceptions, based on our habits and beliefs shaping the reality we encounter.

When we take on the task with new eyes, we recognize the futility of continuing to approach in the same manner. We stop pushing. We choose specific action instead. In time, we will notice a vivid change in our perception. With our persistence, the obstacle has become less onerous.

The wall hasn't changed, we have.

It's similar to our response to certain household tasks. Raised by a mom who despised cleaning and loved resistance as a form of rebellion, I had some intensely ingrained habits-of-thought. Her children were bound to pick up this trait and so resistance became my go-to method for any chore deemed unpleasant.

The laundry would be avoided. The clutter would pile up. The unmade bed would become a tangle of sheets.

Yet all this did was make the wall seem onerous, looming over me, taunting me with the *chores that must be done*. Then I'd power through, patting myself on the back for how I had taken on an overwhelming task. A workload made difficult only because I'd let it pile up. One of the painful yet hilarious jokes we unconsciously play on ourselves all the time.

So I retrained myself to simply do without thought. To take care of tasks in auto-mode, without the build-up of negative anticipation which in turn triggers resistance. As a result, most of the time I barely notice. It's an automatic thing. The Wall that once towered in front of me has shrunk in emotional proportions. In time, I was able to incorporate a true sense of pleasure where resentment once dug in with pointed claws.

This shift in perspective has another distinct reward.

We release judgments.

Hopefully this is now familiar territory. We now recognize when we harbor a trait that secretly bothers us, we judge the trait in others. So we may unconsciously judge those who display a similar trait or who reflect the opposite trait. In a case like this, I might have judged—without ever being aware of my unconscious inclination—those who were either messy or neat as a pin. We also see how disowning certain aspects of being simply results in attracting people who reflect those shadow aspects back to us. In this particular example, we might draw to us folks who want us to become their caretakers. People may subtly hint we should take up a task they find onerous or unpleasant. For me, this drew folks who complained about their lack of order in hopes I would volunteer to take the burden on myself.

We all have walls where we experience this sense of resistance from past conditioning or lingering beliefs. Yet if we persist, the action becomes easier. The "nature of the thing" hasn't changed. We have. And our power to accomplish, "To Do" has increased.

. . .

SUGGESTED FOCUS:

Pick an activity you normally avoid. It can be an outer task like doing the laundry or cleaning out a closet, or an inner focus like meditating for ten minutes a day. Your avoidance might be creative: an urge to paint or write, or physical activities like yoga stretches or hiking. Whatever the choice, for a set amount of time, practice doing without thinking.

You can set an alarm or a reminder to keep you on track. The key is to act swiftly in order to avoid that moment of decision where the potential for resistance can arise. Even just one week of doing without thinking can make a difference.

AFFIRMATION: <u>I have the power to choose and change my habits easily.</u>

REVIEW:

Once we've tackled the concept of 'doing without resistance,' we can take it a bit further. Write down a list of areas where you experience resistance. It might be simple chores like doing the laundry or vacuuming the house, or responding to an email, or paying the bills. It also could be an urge to explore painting, a desire to plant flowers, a yearning to hike, a craving to write a poem.

Then dig a little deeper.

We all have areas where we experience resistance and avoidance: remaining silent when we should speak up; reaching for a 16 oz. cola instead of sparkling water with a fresh squeeze of lemon; watching TV instead of taking a walk or exploring our chosen art. Goals that we long to accomplish yet still we feel that tug of resistance as if an unseen anchor is holding us back.

Here's where our power of visualization can be utilized yet again.

Invest a few minutes focusing on a goal you yearn to accomplish easily, as if you'd already accomplished the goal and are now looking back with pleasure and pride.

See yourself stretching into yogic poses, or walking briskly around the neighborhood greeting others, or splashing paint on a canvas, or strumming a chord on your ukulele. If you have definitive goals, picture the finish line. It may be typing, "The End," on a story you yearn to write, or plucking a fresh tomato from the garden you hope to plant.

Practice this visualization for a minimum of one week, finishing up with "It feels so good to have accomplished this! It's both easy and pleasurable to..." or any affirmation that supports your vision.

EIGHTEEN
REMEMBERING THE MAGIC

Synchronistic meetings are like mirrors that reflect something of ourselves. If we want to grow spiritually, all we have to do is take a good look. Synchronicity holds the promise that if we want to change inside, the patterns of our external life will change as well.

JEAN SHINODA BOLEN

Synchronicity is one of Jung's most fascinating concepts. The idea so inspired Sting, he composed a song of the same name for an album released in 1983. The concept focuses on the simple yet extraordinary idea that everything is connected. The Oxford dictionary definition reads: *The simultaneous occurrence of events which appear significantly related but have no discernible causal connection.*

As my mind toyed with this fascinating notion, I could flash back to all those moments when this connection was obvious. Suddenly thinking of a long-distance friend only to discover a colorful post card waiting in my mailbox, or hearing the ring of the telephone and instantly knowing who'd be on the line.

Synchronicity is the coming together of inner and outer events in a way that cannot be explained by cause and effect and that is meaningful to the observer. —C.G. Jung

One intriguing example came about in my twenties. At the time, my abode was a large rental house with five bedrooms that amounted to four to five roommates, and my first husband. We tended to have low-key parties fairly regularly since even inviting one guest each turned the evening into a social event. Since my teens, my social hunger leaned towards evocative conversations, stimulating discussions incorporating philosophy, theosophy, metaphysics, psychology, and mythology, along with encouraging folks to spontaneously create stories as a group or engage in spirited word play.

My longstanding passion was (and still is) exploring ideas about dreams, probabilities, and the nature of reality. Recent studies and investigations had me bursting with new ideas, speculations and theories, all of which would enthusiastically pour out of me if offered even a hint of encouragement. At one of our many impromptu gatherings, I became engrossed in a discussion with a fellow named Jason. We talked for a couple of hours, comparing mental notes regarding our theories and personal experiences. Right before he left, Jason turned to me and asked if I'd ever heard of Seth. The name didn't ring a bell, so he informed me that this was an author he thought I'd enjoy, saying, "You and he think a lot alike."

A week later, my husband Bob brought home a box of paperbacks he'd bought at a garage sale and handed the box to me, saying, "Because you like books."

He'd not bothered to go through the contents, nor had I mentioned the conversation shared with the fellow who'd been at our house. Bob simply knew I loved books and that there'd likely to be something in there that appealed to me.

Because you like books.

I do indeed!

Pleased, I pawed through the selection and immediately a book caught my eye: *The Seth Material* by Jane Roberts.

Within seven days, a book mentioned at a party by a new acquaintance was delivered to my hands. My husband just happened to be driving by a garage sale, and happened to pull over. There happened to be a box of books on sale for the bargain price of one dollar, and within that box happened to be a book recommended by a stranger a week before. I'd go on to read many books dictated by Seth through Jane Roberts, and as it happens, synchronicity is a subject favored by the author.

Oh, what a marvelous coincidence!

Those happenstance occurrences really do feel magical yet we're taught to do little else but clap our hands and marvel, not note perhaps this reflection is revealing aspects of a connected undercurrent, a pool of the collective unconscious.

When we label those moments of connection as coincidence, we're defining it as luck or chance, while the idea of synchronicity suggests a deeper intelligence—a collective consciousness that unifies us. We can train ourselves to perceive those connections or dismiss them as merely coincidence.

Discovering respected thinkers like Carl Jung, who'd tracked this chain of thought and formed substantial theories, added considerable substance to those notions dancing in my head in my early teens. Thanks to the brilliant minds before me whose works now add color and depth to these ideas, I began to piece together the realization that life is a waking dream. Indeed all of life appears to be a symbolic representation of our thoughts, feelings, and beliefs.

Noted dream researcher and modern mystic, Robert Moss

stated: *Strings of coincidence can strengthen us in the determination to follow our deepest intuitions, even when they run counter to conventional wisdom and logic and cannot be subjected to rational explanation.*

An intriguing example of synchronicity would be how my current husband George and I came to meet. At the time, I'd been in a long-term relationship of nine years. Although I felt the relationship to be secure and forever, there were unseen cracks running through that perfect bond. My boyfriend was restless and whether I could readily admit it or not, so was I. It was September 23rd, 1995, when a disturbing dream awoke me.

From my notes:

For some reason I was alone. I was sad about that. Walking into my house, someone following me said, "We have to find you a husband."

This shocked me and suddenly I realized that they (?) had somehow separated me from Michael. I was furious. I shouted that I <u>had</u> a life partner, what did I need with a husband? "They" had kept me away from my boyfriend. (While within the dream, the unseen "they" were perceived as my guides.)

I angrily went to the person directly responsible, shouting that they had no right and was then informed that 1-½ years had gone by. I was confused. Was my memory blanked out or what? I repeated that, 'One and a half years! He's probably already moved on, fallen in love and now I've lost him!" I felt total loneliness and despair. <u>I woke</u>.'

As might be expected this dream unnerved me and seemed really incongruous. As far as my conscious mind was concerned, all was well between us, so what could this be about? Little did I know that my sweet boyfriend was itching for new experiences. In short order, he'd have an affair with a fellow actor and in January, hand me a letter where he apologetically explained his actions while realistically noting that his affair was the symptom of greater issues that needed to be resolved.

Flashing back again to September, the time of my dream, I'd recently sent a letter to Rob Butts, the husband of Jane Roberts, author of the Seth books, and he'd responded. My continuing interest in the Seth material had instilled within me a desire to take the next step, to connect with others who shared my fascination for exploring these stimulating ideas about the nature of reality. Rob had written back with information about a magazine called *Reality Change*, along with contact info for the publishers. Following my conversation with the two fellows who published the magazine, I discovered within the internet halls of CompuServe a forum focusing on Jane and Seth, and even better, a conference coming up, April of 1996.

While chatting on the phone, I needed something to jot down notes so I grabbed my dream journal, and flipped the page. I scribbled the relevant information there.

After the shocking pain of his big reveal in January, my boyfriend and I would spend the next few months trying to fix a relationship that had run its course. We'd invest in counseling yet even there the counselor privately advised me to face facts, Michael was ready to move on whether he could admit it or not. Sometimes relationships need to end and it's better to recognize this rather than continue to act out destructively to create an escape route. I recognized the truth in this quite dramatically when I discovered evidence that he'd been attempting to reconnect with the woman with whom he'd had an affair.

April rolled around and off I went to the conference, accompanied by a female friend who would be sharing the room. When I first shook hands with my future husband, his name seemed vaguely familiar. Later I realized that he'd actually left the CompuServe forum within a week of my joining. He'd responded to one of my posts and then vanished, though I'd been able to scroll through some of his earlier discussions in the forum.

The next night though, we shared a glass of wine while chatting and just clicked. The intense energy between us was uncanny. I'd never experienced such an extraordinary connection nor felt such an urgency to know someone. The idea of 'falling in love at first sight' has always struck me as deliciously romantic but ultimately unrealistic.

The rippling undercurrent was a ribbon of fire carving a path between us. We felt bonded, as if our souls were coming home. Clearly this situation dove deeper than our reasoning minds could comprehend.

When I returned home though, back to the reality of my long-term boyfriend, my reaction was to send him a note stating that the powerful attraction between us made friendship too risky for me. My relationship was precarious enough without throwing this into the mix.

Much to my surprise, my boyfriend encouraged me to stay friends with this fellow even though I'd admitted an intense pull. When I pointed out the risks—I could see myself falling in love with this man—he not only was willing to take that chance, he seemed to encourage it.

It was time for us to move on, but we had loved each other too much and for too long to accept that fact easily. Even though he'd struggle mightily when the end ultimately arrived, on an inner level, my boyfriend knew we were over, as did I.

Now, the reason this story is significant is because my husband and I did fall in love, did get married, and were together so quickly it was almost surreal. Yet the strange part is this:

The chain of events that led to our getting together was a phone number scribbled down *one day after my dream*.

I still have that dream journal, and the proof of this incredible synchronicity jotted on the back of a page.

Coincidence?

Or a synchronistic event that appears meticulously sketched out by an unseen hand?

"We have to find you a husband."

The timing within the dream was not exact. It would be half a year and one month, not a year and a half, yet the other details lined up.

Yesterday they called it coincidence. Today it's synchronicity. Tomorrow they'll call it skill.

—Antero Alli

Lately, I've been trying to reconnect with what I know in this regard. This begins with paying more attention to even minor acts of synchronicity. Sometimes random occurrences are less than desirable, to put it mildly. Yet what if I shift my perspective? Now instead of seeing the situations as potential problems they become opportunities I have yet to understand. These unexpected diversions may provide meaningful insights or be productive and purposeful. Yesterday was a good example.

After a long wintery day of running errands, I'd finished roaming the aisles of my local grocery stop—grabbing cans of soup, fresh tomatoes, fragrant bread—then paid the bill and began wheeling my cart out of the store. I reached into my jacket pockets, prepared to slip into my cozy winter gloves and came up one short.

Rather than being upset at the delay, I trusted. *There was a reason* and my glove was not lost—it had slipped away for a purpose not yet discovered. I turned my full cart back around, first glancing over to the customer service desk (not there) then roved up and down the aisles with eyes open, patiently looking for the wayward glove. As I strolled past the meat department, I suddenly remembered I'd forgotten to purchase the free-range chicken. Which just happened to be tonight's main course.

I thought, "Okay, so *that's* why my glove came up missing. Now I've remembered to pick up the chicken, and so the glove can reappear."

In full confidence, I scooped up the package of chicken and slipped it into a plastic bag, ready to return to the checkout counter at the front of the store and buy my one last-minute item. Sure enough, the wayward glove was now perched in plain view at the customer service desk. I purchased the chicken, happily reclaimed my glove, and then slogged my way through the pounding rain to my waiting vehicle. Thanks to the traveling glove, I'd saved myself the need to race back to the store for a forgotten item.

There was a reason.

Obviously that example wasn't as dramatic as The Dream, nor was it particularly life-changing. Examples of synchronicity *should* be as abundant within everyday occurrences as they might appear to be during an incredible event that turns your perspective upside down or even seems to alter your entire existence.

Synchronicity may pop in, nudging you to meet the love of your life or help you suddenly recall a forgotten item on a grocery list.

It's all connected.

This is exactly the way life can feel when we recognize (and remember) that the universe is comprised of consciousness —and we are an integral, beloved part of this universal consciousness. Everything *is* connected, yet we may forget to remember. Some of us have yet to consciously and consistently focus on this, as we've never before taken notice of the delightful connection within all of reality. Those seemingly random coincidences can actually feel like little bursts of magic, just like those delightful tales in the storybooks we cherish.

We can and should remember that life is mystical and that all of us are part of the magic. We can train ourselves to pay attention and notice how often serendipitous clues appear to nudge us, to guide us, when we have eyes and ears open, and a mind trained to pay attention.

Fiction author Charles de Lint said, "I do believe in an everyday sort of magic -- the inexplicable connectedness we sometimes experience with places, people, works of art and the like; the eerie appropriateness of moments of synchronicity; the whispered voice, the hidden presence, when we think we're alone."

The goal is for us to remove the mysterious grandeur of the idea of synchronicity and open up our awareness to allow the idea to become central in our life. We must strive to remember the everyday magic and the whispered intuition that guides us.

SUGGESTED FOCUS:

Let's begin the practice of paying attention to the random coincidences. Many folks begin by noting the synchronicity of glancing at their phone and repeatedly seeing significant strings of numbers: 1:11, 2:22, 3:33, and so on. For me, the numbers popping up on my phones can often be my birthday or birth year. Yet there are so many fabulous synchronistic occurrences that can play out.

Do you think of a song and then it's playing when you walk into a store? Note if a thought pops up right before someone says the exact thing. You may think of a place you lived, then a car drives past with a license plate from that state. If you can, write down or add a note on your phone about the everyday synchronicities as they arise. You may be surprised at how quickly they add up. Once when my husband and I were on our way to an appointment we noticed a strange string of coincidences all connected to the town we'd just moved away from.

A car drove by with a dealership tag from the town, a couple in the bank were discussing the same town, and then through the window we spotted a landscaping team and the logo on the truck revealed the company name matched our former location as well. All very ordinary coincidences to note. Yet the practice of cataloging those everyday synchronicities is vital. It's in this daily practice that we train ourselves to open our intuition, to **notice** *what otherwise might slip innocuously past.*

Spend at least one week noting every synchronicity no matter how mundane. It can be something as ordinary as thinking of an old movie, then stepping into an elevator and hearing a conversation that references the same flick.

AFFIRMATION: I tune into the rhythm of the universe: she provides whatever answers I seek.

REVIEW:

Write a list down of every synchronicity you can recall, whether they are dramatic and life altering or just an ordinary "Huh" moment. As you go through your list, remind yourself that such occurrences of everyday magic are a natural occurrence in life and you are inviting your awareness to expand and note all synchronicities.

Many people think the only synchronistic evidence that matters are events that are intense and over-the-top, a belief that can hold us back. Tuning into our intuition and learning to listen to the whispers of the universe can become a daily practice that enhances all of our life, whether the moments are ordinary or astounding.

Be sure and note anytime you "felt" a nudge and ignored it. What were the consequences?

If you recognize that a word or symbol pops up frequently, or specific numbers or even colors appear in a string of instances, note that as well. By keeping a notebook dedicated to examples of synchronicity or everyday magic, you'll be startled at how simply paying attention will enlarge that experience.

Whenever you see a repeated occurrence, jot it down. You can also explore the idea of the synchronicities symbolically, as if each occurrence happened within a dream. A quick online search can bring up ideas about dream interpretation but keep in mind that symbols can be both archetypal (meaning part of the greater collective consciousness) or personal.

Personal symbols are just that... personal. Someone whose grandmother loved collecting feathers once told me she'd been having doubts about a particular life-changing decision and for about a week, feathers would seem to appear wherever she went. One on a doormat when she stepped out of her house, another on the sidewalk after she left work, and even one floated down when she paused to get a cup of coffee. This triggered a memory of her grandmother advising to follow her heart not her pocketbook. She felt this was a hint to take the offer on a lower-paying job that promised more satisfaction, a choice she made and one that brought her great happiness.

Archetypal symbols are quite powerful and often hint of a particularly significant message. For example, dreaming of a lion can suggest a need to get in touch with your courage or to reach inside and awaken your own heroic self. When in doubt, you can do a quick internet search, examining whether the archetypal interpretation clicks with you.

NINETEEN

FUNHOUSE MIRROR EFFECT

Owning our story can be hard but not nearly as difficult as spending our lives running from it. Embracing our vulnerabilities is risky but not nearly as dangerous as giving up on love and belonging and joy—the experiences that make us the most vulnerable. Only when we are brave enough to explore the darkness will we discover the infinite power of our light.

BRENÉ BROWN

What might occur when we become aware how every wise *or* destructive action we take, every focused thought we clutch, is mirrored back to us?

In 2014, protestors in Kiev took a unique approach. Instead of hand-lettered signs, they held up mirrors to riot police, forcing them to face their own images. When Michael Brown was murdered with gunfire in Ferguson, demonstrators around the country utilized the same approach. A stirring and evocative statement, forcing the police to see their own faces as they battled, often ferociously, with peaceful protestors.

I wonder if there could be a more powerful message than, "Look at yourself." It reminds me of an old biblical tale where a ragged, peaceful minded prophet quelled a raging mob by inviting only those who were without sin to cast the first stone.

So when they continued asking him, he lifted up himself, and said unto them, He that is without sin among you, let him first cast a stone at her. —John 8:7

Self-examination is how we grow.

It doesn't matter if the learning we choose is a dedicated skill like sewing, where we inspect the neatness of each stitch or if we're appraising the personality we've stitched together out of hopes and dreams, triumphs and mistakes.

In life, we may find ourselves so numbed by a daily routine it feels as if much of the day is spent just going through the motions. We respond without thinking. We may drive mindlessly along our daily route without ever noticing the bright blue skies. Similarly we can find ourselves automatically interacting with others without ever noticing how our opinions and our emotions are so often reflected back to us. On a regular basis, we unconsciously seek out those telling situations and specific characters that correspond to our inner expectations and hidden beliefs. This occurs constantly, whether our beliefs and expectations are consciously known or cleverly buried deep within.

When any soul comes to a point of awakening her consciousness, it becomes nearly impossible to not perceive what we now know to be true. Serious effort is required to squeeze shut our inner eyes. We must deliberately choose to block out any pesky newfound awareness. In this sense, ignorance really does appear to be bliss. Once we know better, choosing to ignore our inner awareness requires us to slam shut the windows to our soul.

In my childhood, my mom regularly teased us, sometimes rather cruelly. Ongoing jokes that started with "You're so dumb…" My sister was often the target and at the age of eight, I laughed uproariously too.

And then I grew up.

The idea that I played along with insulting my sister horrifies me in retrospect. Examining piece by piece our past choices can be incredibly discomfiting. As children we blurt out stuff that can make our adult self cringe. The most vivid, disturbing part of self-awakening is owning up to all of our choices. Taking responsibility seems easy in theory yet turning that mirror around and actually facing the times we were casually cruel or unconsciously destructive can be agonizing. Which is exactly why so many people avoid self-examination, and will vigorously invest more energy in denial than acceptance.

The more awake we become on an inner level, the easier it becomes to perceive how our conscious thoughts, hidden beliefs, and outer actions are mirrored back to us. Not to suggest this perception and awareness is a comfortable process. Oh dear me, no. Quite the opposite. Once we own up and take responsibility for all thoughts, actions, and beliefs, the piercing discomfort can rattle our psyches.

My own path of awakening often has me squirming with profound embarrassment. Does my soul blush as painfully as I do?

I forced myself to accept this truth: my inner self and I might indeed arrange a few apparent surprises to keep me on my toes, but the bottom-line remains, *there are no random events, no chance encounters.* So if I find myself squaring off with a person, I must admit (no matter how I may squirm and fervently wish otherwise) they are reflecting back to me a quality of being I now (or once did) unwittingly harbor. It is the judgment of this characteristic that still scrapes unpleasantly against my heart. The character trait is often somewhat distorted and exaggerated—I call this the fun house mirror effect—but it's unmistakable. Sometimes the reflection is the other half of a dualistic trait, which is even more of a challenge to perceive.

Jung named this *The Shadow Aspect*.

Let's now circle back and work again with Jung's concept.

Perhaps we have unacknowledged issues of control. Since our lives are designed to trigger awareness, we would unconsciously seek out people and situations to stir up the issue and bring it to our attention. So we would encounter people who are "out of control" to highlight (and compensate for) our overly rigid need for control.

Often control issues are acted out within parent/child roles.

So I must acknowledge if I choose, consciously or unconsciously, to adopt a parental role, I will automatically attract people who respond with resistance. As the drama plays out, the characters in my shadow play will proceed to rebelliously act out, *defying my control*, with childish glee. As those dualistic traits so often play out, in time I'll likely switch roles and be drawn to personalities who in turn want to control me, to 'parent' me, sternly wagging metaphorical fingers in admonishment.

Another manner in which shadow aspects play out, and can even be useful with a pocketful of insight to draw from, is how they reveal our hidden beliefs. Those psychological traits that we abhor may be neatly tucked away. A person who fears he is lazy, has a deep-seated belief that he is indolent, may drive himself and others mercilessly. Any time that he sees someone who represents this hidden fear, that person is sharply reprimanded or secretly scorned. We very easily project our fears outward. Knowing this, we can utilize those nagging irritations as signposts to lead us towards that hidden belief.

Was it drilled into our heads that silliness is immature and inappropriate? If so, we might become overly stern and contemptuous of those who romp around with gleeful ease. "Look at that idiot," we may mutter at the lone person dancing away at a music festival, never realizing that it's not the dancer but the reflection of that disowned aspect that is irritating us.

For many, trying to achieve a clear understanding of relevant psychological patterns leads to years of therapy. We may invest much time with the goal of seeking out the root cause of a particular issue. We may need to dedicate a number of sessions in order to analyze the nuances of a challenging relationship, or to unearth the hidden shadows of a scarred childhood. This is a traditional method in psychiatric therapy. Get to the root of the issue. This can so often be a fruitful and rewarding journey, but not always.

Some of us find that circling back provides us with insights and understanding and yet the patterns remain. Why is that?

Ironically, the truth is we don't necessarily have to dig up every lingering shadow or struggle to recall distant events to trace the source. We don't have to sift through every childhood memory or seek out answers in past lives to find out why we adopted a particular character trait. It may be enough to identify the characteristic, own it without fear, and then take steps to release and replace the belief.

This takes courage.

An uneasy task at times, and it can feel like a terrifying leap into a void where we must embrace accountability. The easier option we've examined previously is obvious: blame outside circumstances or others.

Yet when we do try to shift responsibility outside of ourselves, our progress will come to a screeching halt. Awareness absolutely requires us to both retain those glimpses into our shadow self, and take whatever steps are required to propel us into a new direction.

When we don't want to move forward, or even fervently wish to conveniently forget what we now know deep down to be uncomfortably true, it creates a schism. We might unintentionally fragment our psyche, trying desperately to un-see what we now grasp with unmistakable and unnerving clarity. I've known a few who have chosen this route and it's a frightening thought. What mind-altering steps must an individual take to deny what we *know*?

In the end, all of our growth, all wisps of awareness, all life-altering awakenings come with a firm responsibility to continue our forward progress. Once the door is open, we can't close it. The price we pay to ignore what we have learned about ourselves is too dear to risk. Instead we should revel in the discovery of our inner self, and even celebrate for there's always one more door beckoning to be flung open. Our souls are always urging us forward, daring us to become our selves.

One very reassuring, strengthening tidbit is this.

When at last an unwanted psychological pattern is revealed we can choose to deactivate the buttons that exacerbate the situation. One method is simply to remain mindful that when irritation or fear arises this is an automatic response, and then pause to examine what is occurring within the circumstance that triggers us. Is this person irritating me, or is the situation reminiscent of a pattern that brings me discomfort?

I can't control others or outer circumstances, but I can examine and modify my response.

As a child, I assumed if anyone looked in my direction it was a bad thing. My response would be either to assume others were judging me based on my belief of being unloveable or would be targeting me, based on the fear instilled by my stepfather. I had to recognize my automatic response in order to deactivate the button being pushed.

The dominating manipulation of the two women with

whom I was closest in my younger years made me predisposed to feel guilt anytime I objected or confronted them. It took time and patience for me to identify and then modify my ingrained response so that I could at last say, "No," or, "That's not okay."

Once we begin the process of identification, an interesting phenomenon occurs. We may end one relationship or friendship, thinking *that's the end of that,* without realizing that it wasn't a singular event. The pattern itself must be dismantled, which means we may attract similar situations where we now must consciously and deliberately make different choices.

Without any deliberate effort, memories may then float to the surface of our consciousness, allowing us clarity and resolution. As we progress, we'll find ourselves circling back, revisiting old patterns in new, varied situations. This affords us the opportunity to now deliberately make fresh choices. It is in this way we discover our truest sense of liberation. In time, we acquire the ability to see the funhouse mirror with new eyes. We can recognize the distorted patterns that once dominated our personality. It is then we can forgive and release. We can realize those souls who once seemed to torment us were also acting out their own patterns.

They fit our life-script.

They were characters in the first act of our life's play. As we take authorship of our story, we can choose to edit out any patterns that no longer serve us. We can find new challenges and relish our blossoming awareness. To consciously compose a new life script is our goal. To open the curtain on a new act, and deliberately choose our new role in life. A delicious and rewarding second act has now begun.

We needn't deny the past, nor revisit it endlessly (as tempting as that can be). Perhaps my fear of saying the wrong thing stems from watching my mom casually wound my siblings, and myself. Yet to blame her for my pattern accomplishes nothing and now that I *know*, it's largely irrelevant. The choice to release my fear is mine to make.

My growth doesn't require my perfection, it requires my accountability. If I slip up and find myself teasing someone (that distinctly uncomfortable pattern from my childhood) I may not always catch myself in the act. Upon reflection, the review might reveal my unconsciously thoughtless choice. That doesn't mean I need to beat myself up endlessly in retrospect either, since that in itself is a destructive act.

The truly constructive choice is to embrace my accountability. Which means I reach out and apologize, stating that my teasing was mean and I'm sorry.

An uncomfortable but necessary step because *I'm not perfect.*

I recognize that mistakes will be made and blunders will embarrass me, but those who love me will accept my flawed self. The first person who must accept me—in all my imperfect glory—is me.

Similarly I must recognize that those characteristics that drive me up the wall are reflecting back to me patterns meant to be recognized. I've set this in motion unconsciously but deliberately by being drawn to someone who is now my mirror. If someone is overbearing, there is either a fear that needs to be released or a pattern I need to break away from.

Remember always that the shadow aspect appears in both ways. A shadow aspect of responsibility means I'll either be defiantly irresponsible (attracting overly responsible people who will challenge me or be my caretakers) or I'll be the one challenging or cleaning up the messes of those who are irresponsible.

With my diminished sense of personal authority, I tended to attract people who would bully me, put me in my place, make me feel small and stupid, or just generally run roughshod over me. While consciously I may yearn for people to encourage, nurture, support, and assist me, my unconscious desires will take priority. These shadow aspects are appearing to deliberately push me into action. By embracing my own authority, in time I can recognize the caricatures and those buttons will no longer be pushed.

Realizing that people who irritate us are reflecting unacknowledged shadow aspects empowers us. The connection itself a mirror, and the mirror has no investment in hurting me, only revealing the hidden aspect.

I don't need to take it personally.

Once I realize that, I'm free.

SUGGESTED FOCUS:

Gently examine a recurring pattern in your life. Is there an irritating personality trait you seem to encounter regularly, in friends, lovers, or within a work situation? Consider how this trait might echo within you, remembering always our self-judgment can attract larger-than-life examples. When we are fearful, we may attract people who appear fearless. When we judge ourselves for speaking loudly, we may encounter noisy people who irritate us.

There are steps to take. Releasing judgment is the first step.

For example: "It's okay for us and for other folks to be loud or unorganized, quiet or organized. A pattern is often simply an unacknowledged habit, and habits can be changed. If I habitually judge someone for being controlling, then I'm judging myself as well."

When I recognize that the other person is responding to the pattern within me, it becomes easier to not take it personally. "What shadow in me is this circumstance trying to help me perceive? Is there a belief I unconsciously adopted as a child that is now being reflected back to me?"

AFFIRMATION: It's easy for me to identify unproductive beliefs and release them.

REVIEW:
  Step One:
  First let's examine the childhood dynamic based on parents and any siblings (or close family members).
  What traits do you remember most vividly? This list will be "My Childhood Dynamics."
  For me the list would start with:
  Father: Absent. A mystery. Not talked about. An ideal that is not realistic. Feelings of abandonment.
  Stepfather: Cruel, scary, overbearing, authoritative. Feeling unsafe and wanting to please him, and gain approval to avoid punishment.
  Mother: Neglectful, disinterested, sometimes thoughtless. As a child, she often made me feel as if my presence was bothersome yet she also clearly loved me within a limited framework of acceptability. She loved that I read and encouraged that. Feeling as if I must be quiet or frequently absent to be loved or accepted. Mom also resented authority figures and picked a man who bullied her. In many ways, she could act like a petulant teen resisting the authority of a parent. Avoids accountability and blames others or the outside world.
  Brother: Very similar to stepfather yet also can be disdainful and mocking. A long-term deep yearning to please him but unable to get validation. Competitive. Prone to rage that scares me into

silence and triggers fear. Narcissistic tendencies such as inability to take criticism, overbearing need for all attention to be focused on him, needs to come off as superior. If attention is withdrawn or his authority is challenged in any way, he will explode. Wants the perks of being an authority figure without having to take responsibility. Avoids accountability and blames others or the outside world.

<u>Sister</u>: Can be manipulative and cunning, seeking support emotionally and financially. Good at inducing guilt whenever challenged (i.e. "If you call me out when I hurt you or act destructively, you don't love me unconditionally which makes you a terrible person.") Incredibly talented, charismatic, and clever. Shone so brightly I worshiped her as if she were a goddess. She too resented authority but utilized guilt as a weapon for control. Lies easily and often. Competitive. Wants the perks of being an authority figure without having to take responsibility. Avoids accountability and blames others or the outside world.

Next step:

Write up a list of your significant others, your closest friends (including coworkers), and all supervisors.

As honestly as you can, write down traits and observations as you did with your initial list. Underline any significant recurring traits. Those traits represent your unconscious patterns.

Step Three:

Now is when we can take steps to change those patterns and utilize the power of visualization to create a new framework.

Recognizing that I have long-term authority issues, an attraction to narcissistic personalities, along with a subconscious need to please, I must also realize that those patterns are as appealing and addictive as a sugary snack when my energy is crashing.

This repeated trait: "Wants the perks of being an authority figure without having to take responsibility," resulted in me taking on the opposite role: "Taking on the responsibility for authority without getting any of the perks (such as respect)."

My initial attraction to those who reflect my shadows will transform the more I allow myself to recognize all aspects of my personality, and release the need to appease my childhood patterns.

It's helpful to remember that every person encountered in our childhood and beyond is similarly struggling with their own unacknowledged issues, their own shadow aspects. They are not "the enemy"; everyone has a psychological dynamic based on many events known and unknown. My mom's issues stemmed from <u>her</u> experiences and encounters. Patterns are adopted and recirculated for generations until the shadows are finally brought to light.

Step Four:
What traits do you admire most?

This is a useful exercise that both helps us to define our goals in love and friendship but also helps us to define who it is we'd most like to be.

As is probably obvious by now, I very much admire accountability. Yet my childhood heroes were keen on avoiding accountability at every step. Why is that?

Simply put, we tend towards an all or nothing game with our shadow aspects. We overcompensate, rather like feeling as if we're veering into another lane, so we sharply jerk the wheel in the other direction. The goal, of course, is to drive smoothly down the road not veering from side to side.

So for me, I must recognize that accountability is a practice that I'm incorporating one step at a time. Yet what's really cool is that we don't need to be constantly vigilant as much as we need to strive to be consciously aware. Once I know that accountability is something that was lacking in my childhood and so I overcompensated by being overly accountable (taking responsibility not only for my mistakes but for the mistakes of everyone around me), I can train myself to recognize the patterns.

If I'm irresistibly drawn to a personality who begins bragging about her ability to dodge consequences, it is up to me to recognize that she is reflecting a long-term pattern, and being her friend is not a choice that will bring me any happiness. I can stop dragging in people to fix, folks who represent the broken bits of my childhood. Instead it's time to say, "I'm ready to heal and create a new dynamic."

TWENTY
OUR FUTURE BECKONS

No pessimist ever discovered the secrets of the stars, or sailed to an uncharted land, or opened a new heaven to the human spirit.

HELEN KELLER

Hope is allowed.

Trust is encouraged.

These days cynicism is often seen as realistic.

Don't be fooled.

Sturdy oak trees have weathered the harshest storms. From a biting winter frost springs the brightest, most fragrant blossoms. Our world will thrive, and our passion will call forth the future we desire.

Hope is allowed.

Trust is encouraged.

We give ourselves permission to listen to the reassuring whispers of love within our souls. We harken to the soft light that inspires. We sway to the steady heartbeat that guides our world.

Our future beckons.
Our souls will respond.
To life.
To love.
To us all.

TWENTY-ONE

OUR HEROIC SELF

I think a hero is any person really intent on making this a better place for all people.

MAYA ANGELOU

Who do I think I am? Exactly whom do I want to be?

Once again I find myself sifting through the puzzle of my life. The years add up, and every new wrinkle affirms that time is passing and indeed I must at last have achieved that childhood goal of being grown-up.

Yet for some of us, it appears that something is missing.

Where are our dazzling challenges and intriguing quests? Rather than being swept away to a school of magic or finding ourselves plunged into adventures of derring-do, most of us simply struggle along. We face the baffling challenges of peer pressure and the uncertainty of life with a personality yet to be formed. We choose masks of personality and adjust ourselves to the world without ever really answering the most pertinent question of them all.

Who am I?

Decades ago, I was part of the house staff at the Oregon Shakespeare Festival. I assisted audience members with tickets, locating seats, and supplying information.

The restrooms are located on the lower floor.

The snack bar is only open during intermission.

Of course, I'm happy to help you find your seat!

The work was pleasant and satisfying—helping people has always been an enjoyable task for me. There would be a flurry of activity before each performance, followed by long periods of inactivity, with a brief flutter of movement during intermission.

As many of us know, time passes more quickly when life is busy. Other than getting absorbed in a book, there was little to do while the actors recited their lines. I remember feeling edgy at one point, restless and eager to do something, anything.

The house manager strolled by and asked how I was doing. I felt a tug of impatience and said, "I feel I should be doing *something.*"

He laughed, commenting, "I know what you mean. It's like we should be saving lives or something."

Nailed it.

Yup. I wanted to be doing something heroic, exciting, meaningful! Not just sitting around reading a book. The reason is simple. We define ourselves through our actions, through our accomplishments. When we're children, we can become involved in life in such a daring, adventurous way we feel validated, even invigorated. Daily tasks just don't have the same pizzazz.

Yet as I gaze back fondly at those endless days I perceive the story within the play. If I edited out every bit of my life-script that didn't live up to my shallow interpretation of heroics, the story would be empty and with little heart.

Perhaps helping a frail elder find her seat wasn't obviously life changing, but a bit of kindness offered to a soul feeling overwhelmed in her excitement can be a quietly heroic choice.

A few years ago, I had the opportunity to meet up with some friends in Kauai. At one point, I excused myself and headed to the restroom. While washing my hands, I exchanged smiles with another woman at the sink. Struck by her presence, I said, "Oh my, you are so beautiful."

To my surprise, she gazed back at me with eyes that quickly filled with tears. Astonished, I reached over and took her hand. She whispered, "Thank you," then went on to explain. She'd been diagnosed with cancer and had been forced to get a mastectomy. Her mother had suggested this holiday and though reluctant, she'd agreed. Just before I'd spoken, she'd been staring at herself in the mirror, wondering if she could ever be considered attractive again.

When she told me, my tears joined hers.

Sometimes it's just being ourselves, consciously and appreciatively within a moment that we have the opportunity to be a hero.

Sadly we often forget that becoming our self, fully and brilliantly, in whatever capacity, in whatever manner, is actually a heroic quest. The you existing now is a unique, amazing contribution to life. Especially when we choose to embrace our quest with the idea that every action, every choice we make, ever word we utter can change someone's life.

Even more vital is to recognize the most important life we change is our own.

When I began my life, the scornful question felt like a slap. "Who do you think you are?" So, let me take on this question personally.

Who do I think I am? Who do I want to be?

I want to be a person of substance, a woman of vision with clarity, compassion, and a good measure of self-awareness. That's a good start. We all have the capability to choose who we want to be and become our own heroes. Those qualities we admire in others are admirable because deep within we yearn to acknowledge similar characteristics within ourselves. Yet we don't recognize those stirrings and may even feel discomfort at the idea.

"We ask ourselves, 'Who am I to be brilliant, gorgeous, talented, fabulous?'"

Marianne Williamson posed this question within a brilliant piece written many years ago. Her answer pierced through my fears, illuminating like a burning candle on the darkest night.

"Actually, who are you not to be?"

When I first read her poem, over two decades ago now, I burst into cathartic tears. As a child my heart had been squeezed into the narrowest definition of selfhood. I felt bound up tightly in fearful assumptions and suddenly, her words burned away the cords holding me prisoner.

Gratitude and relief surged in, cleansing away the lifelong shame of simply being me. All those years of hiding my light, being slapped down by competitive people who insisted my brightness was an insult. Why shouldn't I, couldn't I be the best I could be?

I still feel a debt of gratitude to the author whose words unlocked the chains of a lifelong fear and set me free.

We all must start with the same questions: *Who do I think I am? Who do I want to be?* The answers are ongoing and one way to discover those answers for ourselves is to observe what we most admire in others. Chances are good those qualities lie within us like fertile seeds just waiting to sprout. Feed those hopes and cultivate the dreams. Our truest selves are yearning to blossom. It begins now.

SUGGESTED FOCUS:

Choose a quality you admire in others. Consider how that quality might actually lie dormant within your own Self. If you saw this quality in another, just yearning to be acknowledged, what might you do? One way that we become our own best friends is by encouraging ourselves. Look for evidence of that quality within yourself then speak it into being. "I Know that I Am..." Let's begin today.

AFFIRMATION: <u>I choose to recognize that my life is a heroic quest of becoming my truest self.</u>

REVIEW:

This exercise will take place over four weeks. On your start day of the first week, write down a list of five qualities you admire in others. It can sometimes help to write conversationally: "I love how Amanda speaks her mind," "I love that Greg always seems so comfortable in a crowd." "Grace is always so kind," "Sam really knows how to listen." "Tina is so confident!"

Then break it down to qualities of being.

1. *The ability to speak up.*
2. *Feeling comfortable in crowds.*
3. *Being kind.*
4. *Able to listen.*
5. *Confidence.*

Next rewrite the list as if you're listing your own qualities of being. Remember, what we admire and dislike most in others are the shadow aspects within ourselves. Think of these as dormant seeds within you that require both the light of your attention and the nurturing of each drop of encouragement. You will then read this list out loud.

1. I have the ability to speak up.
2. I feel comfortable in crowds.
3. I am kind.
4. I am able to listen to others.
5. I am confident.

Take your time as you read your list aloud, and focus on seeing yourself in situations where you are actualizing those qualities you admire. If there is a past incident you can rewrite, imagine yourself back within that event but now with this newly awakened quality of being. Jot down any feelings that arise. If there is a future event you are anticipating, visualize yourself in action with your quality of being firmly in place. At the end of the week, note changes in your response and your emotions. Be patient with yourself. This exercise is ultimately empowering but like a child learning to ride a bike, you may at first feel awkward or uncoordinated. Honor any fears that arise and practice writing down assurances to yourself, as if you are your oversoul.

In your second week, you can choose to continue with your same list, or write down new qualities you wish to awaken and integrate within yourself. Give yourself four weeks to work with this practice, though it is recommended as a regular habit to continue throughout your life.

PART FOUR

SELF-AWARENESS: CHOOSING TO BE MY AUTHENTIC SELF

TWENTY-TWO
WITHOUT APOLOGY

Again I ponder,
again I ask...
Who do I think
I am?
What emotions arise within
if I dare
to whisper,

I am
brilliant,
beautiful,
glowing with effervescent stars
dancing within
my soul.

I am
hopeful and yearning
for flickers of life
to appear in every
dream
that illuminates my
inner sky.

I am
a wild child
of hope
as soft as
dandelion kisses,
of wishes so
delicate
they taste like
summer dew.

I am
All That Is
within human form,
a living molecule in a conscious
    universe,
who yearns,
creates,
and loves.

I am
Me,
without apology,
determined and curious
with a passion that sweeps away
doubt,
and inspires a life
worth living.

Who do I think I am?

Whoever
I choose
to be.

Who are you?

TWENTY-THREE

WE MUST BE THE HEROES WE SEEK

We do not have to become heroes overnight. Just a step at a time, meeting each thing that comes up ... discovering we have the strength to stare it down.

ELEANOR ROOSEVELT

Truth and lies, falsehoods and fabrications.

Why is it so challenging for us to be honest, not just with each other but with ourselves? How have so many of us become numb to the voice of conscience?

When I was a child, it appeared to me that storybooks were designed to train us to become better individuals. Lessons were woven into plot lines. They cleverly taught us to be courageous in the face of danger, to be accountable in our deeds, to be consciously aware of the consequences of all choices. We learned to be kind and to know that kindness can and does have a positive impact on the world, and so much more. Some were sappy, and often there was a push towards morals, which may or may not sit well depending on one's perspective. Still, authors like Dr. Seuss, Virginia Lee Burton, L. Frank Baum, and Watty Piper, among countless others, offered up delightful, intriguing tales to lift our minds to new heights, open our hearts, and encourage us to create a better world.

Remember *The Little Engine That Could*, by Watty Piper? Such a brilliant story created to teach children the value of optimism and hard work.

The rise of the "anti-hero" deeply altered our collective mindset. Shows like *The Shield* or *The Sopranos* presented us with deeply flawed personalities who were seen as heroic despite their cruel, abusive, violent ways. Reality shows on TV highlighted supposed real personalities who similarly displayed the worst humanity might offer.

It's all fun and games when anti-heroes stir up trouble in scripted show, but when they leap off the screen and seem to appear in our everyday lives, the damage is no longer fictional but rooted within reality. Every person must choose to be honest with themselves and to recognize that being true to ourselves requires us to be accountable, even with little actions that appear inconsequential. Those teensy acts of cheating on our own integral moral codes begin to add up.

I think in many cases, the stepping away from conscience begins innocently enough. We don't want to hurt someone's feelings or we feel obligated to please others so we swallow our feelings. Or we find gain in a seemingly innocent deception that appears harmless. When we stop being accountable to ourselves, the rest just falls into place.

Better to say, "No," with honesty, than "Yes," out of fear, guilt, or obligation.

There's this snippet of a scene from the classic sitcom *Friends*, where Ross is moving and he sees Phoebe and calls out, "Hey, Pheebs, I'm moving, can you help?"

She responds with genuine regret, "Oh! I wish I could but I don't want to!"

She's one of my favorite mythical heroes.

Today, like many recent days, we're faced with dubious authority figures. Folks who've grown accustomed to lying, comfortable with deceit, and sadly, with hearts that appear closed to any whisper of conscience.

Those heroes whose quotes we share time and again would all agree on one thing.

Change begins with you, and with me.

If we want a better world, we must be examples of the change we yearn to see. Awhile back, I caught a bit of pop gossip. Apparently, Brad Pitt had apologized to Jennifer Aniston for the pain and heartbreak he caused her. According to him, her response was, *There are no regrets, only lessons.*

We may be in the midst of one of our greatest lessons in our collective world. This is a time for heroes to arise and challenges to be met with firm resolve.

The insight I've gained of late is this: there is no more time for excuses. No benefit to be gained from self-deception. We must all embrace the courage displayed by fictional heroes, like Harry Potter or the Cowardly Lion, and face up to our conscience, no matter how embarrassing.

Those who are lost must find their own way home. Screaming at them won't help. Ridiculing or condemning them accomplishes nothing.

In May 2017 there was a deadly attack in Portland, Oregon. The news story devastated many of us and held a pointed lesson for me. Taliesin Myrddin Namkai Meche and Rick Best were killed, and Micah Fletcher seriously injured on the MAX light-rail train while defending two young girls from an enraged person that felt nothing but hatred and fear. As Taliesin lay dying, his last words were, *Tell everyone on the train that I love them.*

Can we be as brave as this fallen hero? This was a man who gave his life and never veered from love, even when faced with hatred and with death.

We must be.

Stand in love. Be accountable with your self and with others. Stay informed but stay in love. Those who lash out are broken beyond our ability to comprehend—hating them accomplishes nothing and leaves us with ashes of bitterness within our souls. Worse yet, it turns us away from our hearts.

The healing of our world depends on hearts that believe.

Your heart.

My heart.

Together.

We must never give up hope. Nor turn away from utter accountability. We must be the heroes we seek.

SUGGESTED FOCUS:

Heroes come about because they choose to be the best version of themselves. Some are heroes because they risk life or limb to help others. Yet there are opportunities every day to be quietly heroic. Pausing to help another, returning a shopping cart in the pouring rain, holding back to let a waiting car enter a lane, smiling in sympathy when a frustrated parent struggles with a crying child, scooping a piece of trash and tossing it into a bin.

When we recognize we all have the ability to be kind, helpful, considerate, and useful in dozens of ways daily, we must choose to either act on the impulse or ignore it. Let's choose action. Let's respond as Everyday Heroes and be accountable in our choices.

. . .

AFFIRMATION: <u>I have the power to choose to be a hero every day, and I so choose.</u>

REVIEW:

Spend one week seeking out ways to be an Everyday Hero. Choose little acts of kindness at work, at home, and out and about in the world. Pay close attention to how others respond, even when the reactions aren't what you hoped for or expected. Each day, record in your notebook your chosen acts of kindness along with the responses.

Once I was tossing groceries in my cart when I came across a frazzled mom and her screaming young daughter. The mom was clearly at her wit's end, "If you don't calm down, we'll have to leave and then we won't have food for supper!"

I hesitantly approached and just as I used to do when working at a preschool, I began redirecting the child's focus, commenting on her pretty pink jacket and asking her favorite color. This distracted the child and the more I engaged her, the more she calmed. Soon the mom was able to drift away, smiling a thank-you with her eyes.

Another time in a parking lot, I saw a woman frantically trying to catch a runaway dog about to dash into the street. Even though I was in a hurry, I paused to help rescue the scamp and prevented what might have been a heartbreaking loss.

In both instances, the opportunity arose and I chose to "accept the mission," and the reward was simply knowing I helped another in an ordinary way.

Yet there have been plenty of times I've held open doors, only to have people walk through without giving me a second glance. What then?

This is why it's mandatory that we note all responses,

because sometimes the greatest act of kindness we can offer is the benefit of the doubt.

That grumpy cashier, the sneering customer, the impatient customer service representative, all have stories within their hearts. What if they're struggling because of money worries, or the health of a loved one? What if today is the anniversary of a terrible memory? What if...?

So the next step with this exercise is to note the reactions that were not grateful. Putting yourself in the shoes of another, jot down those 'what if' circumstances and then take a moment to surround the memory with a feeling of supportive love saying, "I hope whatever troubles you is soon healed or resolved."

TWENTY-FOUR
OUR CHOICES DEFINE US

It is our choices, Harry, that show what we truly are, far more than our abilities.

J.K. ROWLING, HARRY POTTER AND THE CHAMBER OF SECRETS

Within every situation a potential insight sparkles. Flickering on the edge of consciousness, understanding beckons. The circumstances, the people, even the entertainment we are drawn to, all reveal aspects of our being.

Our choices define us.

It is within our choices that we discover our beliefs. Beliefs are our means for creation in life— the hues chosen for self-expression within a physical reality. To paint a different picture may require a more expansive or more finite palette. As we pick and choose among the many colors, we discover, bond with, and *become* our Selves. Our consciousness emerges from a combination of yearning to know ourselves and to simultaneously express and experience ourselves.

Any time we experience frustration or dismay, there is a potential for understanding.

Like a waking dream, the symbols we attract reflect a story. Our story. This is what fairy tales and ancient myths represent. A collective story, an archetype that resonates with a common belief—a popular hue on the collective palette. The original longing, when first was uttered the phrase, "Why am I here?" is eternal. In each and every moment, the question resurfaces and can be a useful lens for achieving clarity in any given moment and within life.

Long ago, a friend mentioned how she was dating a wonderful fellow but had serious reservations about his schedule. Work required him to be gone two weeks every month. Two weeks on, two weeks off. I remember distinctly how she mused, "What is it within me that might be drawn to a man who would be gone for weeks at a time? What am I trying to tell myself?"

Those questions led her to examining her own need for independence and space. To recognizing how she was intuitively drawn to a man who automatically filled the unspoken need.

Yet what if the need is less than desirable?

For a number of reasons, everyone develops emotional patterns, which are then reflected in our physical environment. Our beliefs become mental and emotional habits, and as comfortable as old shoes. They fit so nicely and are so familiar we may not recognize exactly what any particular comfort zone is all about. A child neglected or abused might unconsciously be drawn to people or circumstances reflecting a similar pattern. As we explored in Chapter Sixteen, we do often 'marry' our parents, or recreate our childhood for better or worse.

So, "Why am I here?" If I'm not happy with this particular

circumstance, then I need to reflect—has it happened before? If yes, then why did I put myself here again?

How does this circumstance serve me?
What is it I'm trying to tell myself?
What might I hope to learn?

Though finding the source of our beliefs—digging into our past or rooting around in our subconscious—can be useful, it's not required. An absolute necessity is tuning into what this choice means to us *now*. The present moment is always our point of power. We need to examine the circumstance or relationship or pattern with the same objectivity with which we'd explore fictional events.

Why did the heroine in the story make a particular choice?
What did Harry Potter learn?

If we do this, if we encourage our courageous Self and embrace our own derring-do, we can gain enough clarity to say, "Yeah, this isn't serving me at all." It may indeed be time to release this pattern/belief and move forward.

Yet we often find letting go of a pattern/belief, one as comfortable as a snuggly, worn t-shirt, may be challenging in unanticipated ways. A sense of resistance and various emotions may arise unbidden—fear, panic, grief. A feeling of loss can loom like a menacing shadow. This makes no sense *consciously*. On an inner level, there is always much more going on.

One of the most intriguing aspects of letting go is not often touched upon. Many of us become so attached to beliefs, situations, relationships, emotions, even pain, that the mere idea of release can trigger a deep sense of loss.

Psychologically speaking, those aspects of being, whether outer (as in people or situations) or inner (beliefs, emotions, or a state of mind such as martyrdom arising after being stalwart through periods of suffering) become part of our psychological make-up. The "pain" sets us apart. The trying circumstance may offer a feeling of triumph or victory. Our worries, discomfort, physical afflictions, trials and tribulations become a badge of honor, and proof of our validity in one way or another. The troublesome relationship with family or friends may provide unconscious proof of our compassionate nature.

"Look at all I put up with! What a good person I must be."

This is proof we would not need if we were certain we truly were compassionate.

What we consciously bemoan has now become a fixed and valued part of our identity. Even though we consciously believe we'd like to discard this troublesome pattern, there's an underlying resistance based on an emotional identification. The pattern has become part of our psychological make-up. It's become a part of our self.

So there's a definite necessity to recognize the reality of the emotional pay-off. We then take steps to identify and acknowledge it. Finally we work up the courage to be willing to completely release it.

A little recognized insight is that we form attachments to every aspect of our being. Our patterns and beliefs form our psychological make-up. This means there may indeed be a profound sense of loss when we finally discard those aspects of being. The sense of loss, bordering on bereavement, should be honored.

It's not only okay, it is healthy and natural to grieve for those scattered bits of Self we're casting aside. You can even send tender love, compassionate support, and soothing comfort to the old 'you' who is also being (in an eerie way) discarded. We *should* be gentle with our growing selves, always offering love and encouragement, support and comfort.

When I was in my late teens, a very pregnant stray cat wandered into my life. This was my first experience with witnessing the miracle of birth and I adored those teensy

Siamese kittens that tottered on wobbly legs and meowed with such power. I had no clue of the ways of nature so what occurred during the weaning process shocked me to my core.

Every time a kitten would approach the formerly sweet and doting mama cat, she'd snarl fiercely and smack them away. It horrified me and shook me. Obviously my own insecurities, my fearful shame of feeling like an unwanted child rose like bile, choking me with emotion.

I had to force myself to realize she didn't hate them, she wasn't hurting them. This was a natural process (even if horribly uncomfortable to witness), a purposeful action to force the kittens away.

There's a similar process that occurs when a long-term relationship runs its course and yet there is deep attachment. Some have the capacity to move into objectivity and strive for an amicable break-up, yet others subconsciously choose destructive acts or words to force a break in the bond. It can happen with jobs we hate or circumstances we abhor as well.

When we choose a different course, emotions arise that may seem out of synch. We hated that job so why are we still so upset over being fired? The obvious reason may be those feelings of injustice or indignation, believing we weren't valued, and feeling betrayed. Mingled with the anger is often an unacknowledged grief over losing something valued.

Even when what we valued was not in our best interest.

When we choose to change aspects of our personality or to grow into a new perspective, we're opening doors and stepping into new territory ripe for exploration. Yet once we grow into a new phase, we're also releasing the old. An unhappy ending does not mean the beginning wasn't once sweet. The butterfly testing her wings may well feel occasional grief and longing for the caterpillar she once was.

And that's okay.

Not only okay, it's natural and healthy.

So as you grow into your new sense of self, as you work through the qualities of being you wish to incorporate, as you sift through worn-out beliefs and exchange them for stronger, healthier and more fulfilling choices, you may feel unexplained loss. Honor that within you and allow yourself to reflect on those changes.

Aspects of self die and are reborn continuously throughout our lives. Tucked within every twilight is a new dawn.

SUGGESTED FOCUS:

Once again, we're going to practice objectivity from the perspective of our oversoul. If during the course of your exploration, you find yourself dealing with unexpected grief, sit down with your notebook and pen an encouraging love note to yourself.

"Hey you... Just want to remind you how sweetly you are loved. I know it hurts to let go, yet honestly We no longer need that pattern/belief. Look at how much we've grown! It is time to release now and move into a new phase."

AFFIRMATION: The present moment is the point of power and so I release the past and allow my past self to heal so I may live fully in my present moment.

REVIEW:

In your notebook, note any significant transitions in your life and the emotions that arose. For some people, certain time periods—such as the high school years, beginning a new project, starting a family, or even being a specific age—were particularly satisfying. What emotions arise when you review that time? If there is grief or longing, it's time to honor that.

Write out a tribute to your past 'self,' where you honor the self you were at the time. This can be as expansive or as brief as you choose. If you have a photo or memento, place that within your view. Allow yourself to experience your emotions fully and be sure to record whatever arises during this exercise.

Next, pen a thank-you letter to this 'self' and ask them to remain in your life as a guide and even a cheerleader when you need a boost. It can be helpful to choose a nickname for that phase that you can utilize when you wish to ask for support.

TWENTY-FIVE
OUR LENS OF REALITY

We don't see things as they are. We see them as we are.

ANAIS NIN

In previous chapters, we've delved into the concept of how psychological patterns attract experiences and relationships. We are drawn to souls who reflect our disowned shadow aspects specifically because reality is designed to prompt us towards self-awareness. Yet because of past experiences, childhood events, and conditioning absorbed culturally or personally through family, friends, and observations, we form beliefs about what reality is and what it isn't. We're going to revisit this concept because it's the most vital notion we can consider.

Our reality is formed by our beliefs.

Beliefs differ from opinions in that we incorporate the belief into our notion of reality as if it were fact. An actual fact is that the earth rotates and because of this we experience daylight when the globe is facing the sun and evening when the sun disappears from our view. Yet personality is formed out of beliefs such as *I chatter when nervous* or *I thrive on new experiences*. These beliefs may seem like facts because we've accepted them so firmly they appear to be inconvertible.

Beliefs are the mainstay of our experience. Even if one were to discount the notion of beliefs forming the fabric of reality—a concept being explored and supported by today's physicists—it is clear that beliefs have a definite and obvious impact on our perception.

Perception, at the very least, is our unique individual lens of reality.

To understand how this works, imagine a magnifying glass highlighting all of your "belief evidence." A handy tool, yet one with a distinct disadvantage. We grow so used to the view perceived through this lens of belief, that we forget there may be other views available. This handy-dandy tool becomes our go-to means of examining the world around us. Which makes it incredibly challenging to perceive contradictory belief evidence unless we consciously set the lens aside.

So we use our easy-to-grab mental magnifying glass to zoom in on factors that reinforce those hidden beliefs we hold dear. The beliefs can be healthy or destructive, pleasing or terrifying. The magnifying glass has no investment either way. It simply zooms in on the reality we *choose* to believe in.

Here's an example of one of my more positive early core beliefs: *Deep down, everyone is good.*

Now this belief may have been in part a survival mechanism, allowing me to retain a degree of love and faith despite emotional challenges in my youth. In an abusive or neglectful environment, a young child desperately needs scraps of hope. If instead I believed that everyone was bad, my fearfulness would have overwhelmed my spirit.

In many ways, this is a good and satisfying belief which

served me well, and yet when unexamined had unexpected consequences. It took decades before I recognized this wonderful and loving belief could be used as a smokescreen to ignore bad behavior or permit callous souls to hurt me, time and time again. So perhaps a better, more evolved belief would be: *Deep down, everyone is good. Yet if the choices they make are destructive or hurtful to me, it's okay to keep a loving distance.*

All beliefs can evolve.

All beliefs *should* evolve.

They're basic patterns as distinct as a paint-by-numbers set. They serve us well when starting off but eventually we have to take control. We must own the awesome power and heady responsibility of the artistic choices within our lives.

There is incredible beauty in realizing beliefs structure our experience. Those beliefs urged us to choose stalwart or troublesome friends, devoted or temporary lovers, invigorating or frustrating jobs, and all life experiences. Even better is to grasp that all of these beliefs can be modified. This realization is not only liberating, it is life altering.

We may encounter many folks in our lives who insist our beliefs should match up with theirs. People who want to use us to reinforce their own perceptions (based on their beliefs) or who attempt to control us because of their belief-driven views. The freedom for us arrives when we recognize quite clearly we do not need to support or buy into any unhealthy or harmful beliefs.

Beliefs are tools, building blocks of reality.

We use them to construct the life we live.

When beliefs are detrimental or restrictive, they become chains, binding us to patterns; limiting our growth. Life requires us to continue to progress and strive for self-awareness. Whether we like it or not, every pattern and belief will be brought to our attention, by choice or by seemingly unbidden circumstance.

The latter requires us to stumble into events seemingly beyond our control. We'll often attract relationships or even casual encounters as a means of perceiving beliefs tucked neatly away in our subconscious. *The beliefs we hold create our reality.* Whether the outcome is delightful or agonizingly uncomfortable, we all must eventually experience and evaluate the results of our beliefs. That is life's purpose.

How then can we best utilize our "belief lens"?

Whenever an individual or a circumstance gets under our skin, we take a moment to remind ourselves, "This is a belief being magnified for my benefit."

We can then pause and explore, dig a little deeper to see what surfaces as a result.

What emotions do I feel here? What assumptions are arising based on the emotion?

Then we take a vital step and say: *"I believe that..."*

What comes up? *I believe this person is...* Fill in the blank and then ask, how does this make me feel? Perhaps I feel a prickling of fear or frustration. Whatever I believe about the other person is a clue to a pattern within my own psyche. If it's an invigorating belief (*She's so daring! I really admire her!*), what a pleasant thrill to consider this 'daring' is something untapped within myself. A boldness I can embrace and perhaps I'm now ready to do just that.

If the belief is uncomfortable (*He's so pushy, controlling, manipulative*), it is time for some brave self-examination. Does this remind me of a pattern I've encountered in others or... even within myself? Am I fearful of being manipulated? Am I angry at manipulations in my past?

Exploring our feelings and beliefs gives us strength and clarity. We can then choose to acknowledge what this encounter is stirring up, without requiring blame. Meaning, I don't have to be angry or fearful, I can choose instead to walk away. When we attach blame, anger, or judgment, walking away becomes more difficult. When we accept what the situation is teaching us, we can recognize this person is acting out a role in our life and we no longer need to share this particular stage.

One thing we must consider is how our beliefs not only impact our perception of others; they can also lock us into situations. A mild example would be my mom's habit of seeking out situations that annoyed her. Once she told me about a checker at the local supermarket who always, in my mom's words, "Screwed things up." I'd listen to her and then suggest perhaps she could avoid going through that particular checkout line. Mom would listen and half-heartedly agree but seriously, where was the fun in that? I watched her work herself up with passionate indignation, relishing every grievous offense she encountered. Yet there was another side to this reoccurring drama.

When we presuppose the actions or attitudes of others, we may not give them room to be anything else. We seek out proof of our preexisting beliefs, and when that proof is offered, we get the emotional pay-off discussed in previous chapters. The checker who 'screwed things up' may have been upset or hurried or distracted. When she encountered a customer who was giving her *the eye*, who knows what she felt?

I remember quite clearly many times when others held me firmly in the grip of their own predisposed beliefs. Around one friend, I always became unbelievably talkative *just as I did as a nervous child*. She'd often reinforce this with her own comments and sure enough, that's who I felt myself become within her presence.

We form conclusions and oftentimes we find that others respond to those conclusions.

I knew she was unreasonable.
I knew he'd do that one thing he knows I hate.

My belief lens will pick out every circumstance that corresponds to the belief, and pretty much ignore proof to the contrary. An interesting suggestion was brought up in the book, *Nature of Personal Reality*, by Jane Roberts. The idea being that we can visualize outwardly onto other people as well as inwardly, regarding ourselves.

A wife who is frustrated because her boss cuts her off whenever she speaks eventually learns to *expect* this demeaning act to occur. She may indeed speak up, share her feelings hoping for change, but the picture in her mind reinforces the behavior. Just like a hopeful Olympic skier who's taken a tumble must erase that mental picture and replace it with success, so she must take steps to picture a new outcome.

By forming a mental image that differs, we are not only creating an alternate reality for ourselves, we're creating a mental image for others to step into as well.

When my husband and I were first together, his mother and sister made plans to fly out for a family Thanksgiving. I was nervous and excited. My mother-in-law, Dorothy, was a lovely woman who had flown out the year before to meet me and we'd gotten along splendidly. Chatting over dinner and drinks, I genuinely enjoyed her company. There was a bit of trepidation regarding the upcoming holiday as we'd just moved into a new home a few months earlier, and along with shopping for furniture and household items, we'd also moved my mom down from Portland, to Ashland, Oregon, finally giving her a home of her own.

When Dorothy and her son (my husband) began making plans though, there was a rift. She'd invited a distant cousin without checking first and my husband let her know she'd have to rescind the invitation. Our home was small and we were already scrambling to work out arrangements. Needless to say, this bothered her and because of her adoration for her son (with whom she couldn't get mad) she blamed me.

Or tried to.

I could see it clearly. She couldn't be mad at George so she'd be mad at me. Except that I refused to reinforce her anger, or take it personally. I just kept acting like everything was okay, refusing to take his side or hers. *I focused my imagination on seeing it all work out.* Utilizing my power of visualization, I kept my inner eyes on seeing the holiday coming together beautifully without any problems.

The picture in my mind was not going to be changed no matter what occurred prior to the event. I continued to firmly believe my husband was wonderful and so was my delightful mum-in-law and *it would all work out*. At first she tried to engage my anger but her ire didn't fit into my mental picture. Eventually she let it go and that was that. My wonderful mother-in-law found my inner focus an easy fit because she was a kind, loving woman.

This is not a natural talent for me as there were many years when the pictures in my mind, my firmly entrenched beliefs, have overridden my own attempts to create an alternate reality. So it was not only a relief, it provided a rich and satisfying bit of proof that focusing on the outcome I desire gives the other person an alternate picture to step into as well. Often we become so invested in our discontent we don't even leave a space for the possibility of change, so this focus can be useful in that we make room for a new probability to emerge.

Now my example could have gone the other way. Mother and son could have clashed on this no matter how much I focused because they are choosing their probability as well. I drew an outline on a mental sidewalk and they chose to step into that outline, for which I am grateful.

Yet what if people have no interest in that probability?

The truth is that we create *our* reality, not the reality of others. There is collective reality—a shared space—and our personal reality. If someone is unhappy within a relationship, and they write out a list of qualities they yearn to see within a mate, the first step is always to ask, "Have I incorporated those qualities I seek?" Even more vital is the second step: "Is the change I yearn to see in this person a realistic hope?"

What we have to understand is that when we diligently focus on a picture in our mind, change may not occur in ways we expect. A focus on being respected and valued at work may not result in this particular boss changing his tune, but instead may result in us leaving one job and finding another where we feel appreciated.

Feeling frustrated with a lover who betrays us, we may focus diligently on seeing him or her change into a loving, respectful partner, yet if that partner has no desire to fit that role, we cannot force them to change. We may find though that the relationship must end in order for there to be a space for that loving, respectful partner to fill.

However, if our focus on the annoyances overwhelms us, our partner, our boss, our friends may feel locked into expected roles, and so focusing on a more satisfactory outcome sends out an unconscious message that invites change.

It begins with knowing both ourselves and our beliefs. Then we can incorporate the understanding that our job, our friends, and our lovers were brought into our life based on our beliefs.

SUGGESTED FOCUS:

Write down annoyances as if they're beliefs. "He's so manipulative," means I believe I can be manipulated. If I believed firmly that I couldn't be manipulated it would be an easy thing to just walk away. This doesn't mean his nature has changed, but that my belief has made me susceptible to the manipulation. Instead of trying to change the person, which may not be within our capability, I'll examine how and why I let myself believe that I should respond to manipulations. What if I could "just say no"?

AFFIRMATION: <u>I always have power of choice. The more I know my beliefs, the easier my life becomes.</u>

REVIEW:

If there is a particular person or incident that troubles you, write down the situation then add: <u>This is my perception.</u>

Now it is time to create an alternate story. If you are focusing on a person, you must remember you can't change them, you can only change the situation in which they exist. So rather than saying, "Joe is a thoughtful person who respects my feelings," or "Maggie is loyal and kind," reframe it with <u>my friend/lover/boss is thoughtful and respects my feelings.</u>

"I have a partner who is kind."

This exercise does two things. First, as mentioned, it creates a mental outline for others, who then can <u>choose</u> *to step into that new framework you've created. Even more importantly, it changes your beliefs about the other person, which again, allows space for them to change.*

However it's vital that we not utilize this as a means of ignoring or overriding our awareness within a situation. If a lover, boss, or friend is treating me poorly, I must be able to weigh my evaluation of the situation as well as my beliefs. This is particularly vital for those of us who've experienced abuse or manipulation.

Write down grievances on a list and look at them honestly. Then write your list of expectations and evaluate them with a clear eye. Could your partner/friend/supervisor actually change or is it just wishful thinking?

Answer this question: "What does this situation or the actions of this person tell me about my beliefs and my expectations?"

Follow-up: *Write down a list of beliefs that would match up with a fulfilling reality.*

I am healthy.

I am respected.

I am treated kindly.

(follow your heart with this)

TWENTY-SIX
CHOOSING OUR BELIEFS

Your thoughts and beliefs of the past have created this moment, and all the moments up to this moment. What you are now choosing to believe and think and say will create the next moment and the next day and the next month and the next year.

LOUISE HAY

One thing to recognize about our beliefs is even when we incorporate them without a second thought, they are still a choice. An unconscious choice perhaps, which is why we hope to bring those auto-beliefs to light so we can perceive them clearly. Otherwise the choice becomes a habit.

Habits of mind, habits of thoughts. Those habitual beliefs can so often trip us up. It's quite easy to forget, within every moment, reality is created anew.

It's not just that we are *choosing* to have a belief. We are choosing to *reinforce* the belief and will most certainly remind ourselves regularly lest we forget. Let this sink in for a moment. It's as if we unconsciously set a proximity alarm up to warn us if we stray off track. We're choosing to stay within those mental patterns, often simply out of habit.

Brushing our teeth is a habit and after we've done it a few thousand times, it becomes so automatic we can easily go through the motions without even noticing. Reinforcing beliefs is also a habit. We remind ourselves of what we believe constantly without ever noticing.

How many times as a kid did I say, "No," to an unfamiliar food? Only to hear, "How do you know if you won't try it?"

I remember once in my early twenties, hanging out at a jazz club in Los Angeles. After a couple of vodka Collins, I was feeling a bit toasty so asked the bartender if there was any food on the menu. "Cheese and crackers," he told me, so I ordered it along with a cup of tea.

My attention was on the music as I munched on the cheese, until one taste caught my attention. It brought me out of my buzz as my taste buds registered a distinctly unpleasant flavor, which turned out to be Swiss cheese. As my fuzzy brain worked it out, I started laughing.

"This is Swiss cheese! I *knew* I didn't like it!"

Because I'd long judged myself for instinctively not wanting to try Swiss cheese, believing firmly I didn't like it (though in actuality, I'd never tried it). And now I knew.

It could have easily gone the other way. My belief that I didn't like Swiss could have been shattered by this unexpected proof. Often we do set ourselves up to break through a situation, to confront those habitual beliefs.

This is one reason we may create sudden and dramatic occurrences, 'out of the blue'. Sometimes we even encounter catastrophic events to rattle our perspective and occasionally toss us about like a beach ball in a hurricane.

Why did I do this? Why would I create this horrid, wildly uncomfortable scenario?

Why did I get fired, or discover my loved one had an affair? Why do I suddenly have to move, why must I deal with this tragedy, why am I seemingly being forced into a new situation?

One example in my own life I detailed in Chapter Eighteen. My boyfriend's affair threw me out of my comfortable routine and figuratively broke my world apart. Yet, out of the rubble I rose and because of this heartbreak, I was more inclined to view an unexpected encounter with a receptive heart. The unexpected led me to finding love with my husband, a relationship that still nourishes and fulfills us both after two decades.

The unexpected often serves a valuable purpose in assisting us. It helps us to break patterns we've locked ourselves into out of habit.

We're covering what hopefully is now becoming familiar ground. Actually the idea that beliefs create reality is simple enough for one essay, yet understanding this concept often requires we dismantle previously cherished ideas and rebuild our mode of perception. So let's circle around again and examine this idea.

To break it down even further we need to truly grasp that beliefs are not reality itself. Beliefs are our *ideas* about reality. We may believe people automatically like us or automatically dislike us. This belief will then influence not only how we interpret the reactions of others, it will urge us to unconsciously seek out those who will fulfill our expectations. All based on the belief.

If someone frowns we may think, *Oh, they don't like me,* when actually they're fretting about their dead-end job or wondering if the fast-food burger they chomped down earlier was a horrible idea. So we interpret their reactions through a lens of perception created by our belief.

Similarly, we're instinctively drawn to friends, coworkers, lovers who match up with those internal expectations. This is another automatic choice, whether those expectations are ever brought to the light of consciousness or not. Psychological studies teach us many patterns of belief are ingrained in us since childhood. Sometimes the patterns are based on early interactions, or unconsciously absorbed by observing our extended family or circle of friends. When we identify the belief patterns, we can then modify or simply remove and replace any outdated beliefs with fresh beliefs, ones more constructive and beneficial.

The first step in changing our patterns is always to recognize how we hold onto beliefs and how they shape our experience.

Until you make the unconscious conscious, it will direct your life and you will call it fate.

—Carl Jung

We must become consciously aware of the distinction between I *am* my beliefs, and I *have* beliefs.

As always, I'll remind us all, beliefs are the building blocks of our reality. We can rearrange them or exchange them for more useful beliefs that serve a new, more productive purpose in our life. Yet daily routines can be numbing, challenges may be overwhelming and it's just so easy to slip into autopilot, whether we're engaging in the nightly rituals of brushing teeth or driving down the same tree-lined street we've traveled a hundred times before. Habits form based on repetitive actions or thoughts. Every thought pattern becomes ingrained and we may forget how fluid and changeable reality can be. This makes it even more vital to remind ourselves: beliefs are not static, nor set in stone.

We choose to believe.

Each belief is a choice.

In fact, we are in the process of choosing in this exact moment.

Let's examine how we may automatically perceive a belief and how we can modify our perception.

1. I have a belief.
2. I am *choosing* to have a belief.
3. I am *choosing to reinforce the idea* that I have this belief.

It's rather hilarious when we step back and consider. Of course, it's not so much fun when the results of these beliefs appear dire. Not at all entertaining when we feel lost, helpless to release an ingrained pattern creating havoc in our lives.

Words Matter.

Focus matters.

"People like me."

"People don't like me."

Which focus do we automatically select based on our hidden belief? Which person will we unconsciously seek out to fulfill our belief?

It is for this reason I love to utilize playful games like, "And that's a belief!" Because we may ramble on without paying attention simply out of habit. It can be incredibly useful to utilize a magnifying glass to bring clarity to details we may no longer notice.

The game I call, "And that's a belief," is a handy way to pick out hidden beliefs. It goes something like this. Make a statement considered by you to be absolute fact, then add: "And that's a belief."

People like me.

I'm a great cook.

Staying focused can be hard.

I get more tired when I…

It's hard to change.

Nobody likes me.

Too much activity wears me out.

Not enough activity locks up my muscles.

I'm always up for dancing.
I never get sick.
I always catch a cold when (fill in the blank here).
Parking spaces appear whenever I need them.
I'd love to Do This One Thing but I'm...
I always encounter traffic at this time of day.
People go out of their way to be nice.

And that's a belief.

Beliefs are basically habits of mind. Reaching for a stick of gum or tapping our fingers on the table are good examples of innocuous habits, yet how easy are they to change?

I'm going to start walking every day!
No more sugary treats for me!

We make a New Year's Resolution or swear our new routine will begin on Monday. Then we fret and feel defeated if we falter and slip back to our old ways. It can be so frustrating.

Beliefs are habits of mind.

When I was fifteen, I'd developed a habit of saying, "You know," after every sentence. Watching an old interview of John Lennon (who had the same pattern) sharply reminded me of this old practice, discarded long ago. A teenage friend of mine had a similar habit and it was so much easier to notice from the outside.

Isn't it always?

We tend to pick out annoying patterns or recognize fearful shadows in others with much greater ease than we do within ourselves. We can either strive for self-awareness and accountability, taking ownership of all aspects of our being, or ignore the nagging discomfort, pretending we don't notice the similarity. There's always an unconscious jolt of recognition with those shadow aspects. It triggers a pleasurable sense of connection or a shudder of revulsion we can't explain, yet also can't ignore.

Returning to my example with my teenage friend, whenever

one of us said, "You know," the other would repeat it. Since we were in this together, it was an encouraging, respectful reinforcement (though we often broke into gales of laughter). We broke the habit by bringing our focus into the moment and recognizing The Power of Choice.

As I type this, there's a rueful chuckle lingering because it's easy enough to type these words but I can attest it can take practice to be conscious within each moment. I'm so not there!

(*And that's a belief! You know?*)

However, I can be there, and so can you.

Let's return now to beliefs.

When we modify or completely replace those habits of mind, the former beliefs appear completely out-of-place. I've shared bits and pieces of my background yet it still surprises me to gaze back and review what I once believed.

No one could love me because I'm not good enough.

I'm unattractive and when people look at me it's because they're repulsed or secretly laughing.

Some people are just born with talent so I'll never be good at music.

There are also simple everyday beliefs I adopted: *I'm clumsy. I talk too much. I'm too loud. I always say the wrong thing.*

The irony for us is that if we make the effort, we can usually find proof that these beliefs are not fact, yet they've become habits of mind.

Another way for us to examine this is by recognizing that we regularly indulge in self-hypnosis whenever we repeat a belief.

Your beliefs act like a hypnotist, then. As long as the particular directions are given, so will your automatic experience conform. The one suggestion that can break through is this: I create my reality, and the present is my point of power. —Jane Roberts, *The Nature of Personal Reality*.

Repeating and focusing on affirmations (popularized by Louise Hay, the bestselling author of *You Can Heal Your Life*) can be recognized as a form of self-hypnosis—a means of overriding previous programming with new beliefs.

Yet often when we utilize affirmations they don't have quite the impact we desire. It's like slapping on a fresh coat of white paint over a darker stain. The old belief can eventually bleed through unless we strip away the original color. The first step though, is that we have to recognize that: *This is a belief, not a fact.*

However, one of the reasons these beliefs have such a powerful grip is because our automatic acceptance is usually unnoticeable. Just like my silly habit of saying, "You know," it's established in my mind and unless I break through this 'hypnotic state' it will seem like truth.

There's no point trying, I'll just mess it up.

People don't respect me, and why should they? I'm ....

I'll try to start this new habit but it's probably not going to stick.

If I say anything, I'll probably just look like a fool.

And that's a belief.

When we add those four words, we're reminding ourselves that this belief is *not* a fact. We're beginning the process of deprogramming ourselves out of the belief we've hypnotized ourselves into believing is truth.

How many years have we repeated those mantras of misery? Told ourselves repeatedly that we're unable to accomplish what we yearn for most, or that happiness will elude us, or that we're not deserving of love? Those undesirable beliefs have created a pathway in our brains. All those layers laid down by the repeated application of unconscious hypnotic suggestions.

Imagine if there was a doorway there, yet all those layers of paint have obscured it. The illusion of solidity makes it seem impenetrable and we're stuck gazing miserably at this seemingly impervious obstacle. Reminding ourselves that these 'facts' are simply beliefs that can be changed helps us remember we aren't trapped, there is always a way out.

Time for us to carve open a new door.

SUGGESTED FOCUS: Write down a list of your beliefs. This will be an ongoing exercise you will revisit repeatedly throughout life. The topics will expand as time goes on. Let's start with beliefs about age, beauty, wealth, popularity, health, employment, creativity, and love.

Follow the example set in the essay above. At the top of your page write, I Believe:

Let's see what comes up.

And that's a belief!

AFFIRMATION: Change comes easily. I uncover and change my beliefs with ease.

REVIEW:

Your list will grow over time, let's begin now to incorporate a habit of reviewing those beliefs. Choose five and tell yourself you want to begin noticing whenever you reinforce them. One excellent method is to write down three pages, either typed or handwritten, in a stream-of-consciousness flow. Just rattle on about your day, your activities, your frustrations, your hopes, and your worries.

The next day, after you've written your new pages, review what you wrote the day before. Underline every statement that sounds like a belief. Every time you do this, the easier it will get to notice and highlight those casual statements that are actually hidden beliefs.

Activity: Write 3 pages, review yesterday's pages. Write those three pages for a minimum of one week, though aim for at least one month.

Pay special attention to axioms—repeated and casual statements that you make. Sayings or proverbs that we've heard throughout our life can also reflect unconscious beliefs. "The early bird gets the worm." "You can't appreciate sunshine without rain." "All good things come to an end."

One example from my own life is a phrase my mom uttered regularly: "Hard work builds character."

Now that makes perfect sense and seems very positive overall but the underlying twist is "If you don't engage in work that is **hard**, you won't have any character." That can (and did) generate a fear-based belief suggesting that I better make sure and create circumstances to keep "Working Hard" or I'll suddenly become shallow or shifty. Yet what if it's work I love? That certainly wouldn't fit the bill of "hard" so I could very well set myself up to seek out unpleasant jobs to assure me that I'm engaging in hard work.

Another useful method is to utilize a partner to keep you on track with becoming aware of automatic beliefs. Choose someone you trust and ask them to help point out when you state a belief without noticing. Ask them to simply say, "And that's a belief." It's especially useful if the person is willing to be involved in the same practice. Be sure and set limits if you need a break. For example you could say, "For one hour, while we're talking, let's play That's a Belief."

Be aware that feelings may arise, and you must be gentle and supportive of yourself during this process. You are worth it.

PART FIVE

SELF-LOVE: COMING HOME TO OUR SELVES

TWENTY-SEVEN
HERE IS WHERE WE'LL MEET

Here
is where we'll meet,
where the sweet ocean
breeze
mingles with our breath.
Where each word shared
becomes a moment of startling
recognition.
A clarity of heart shining light
where shadows slept.

Here is where we'll meet,
for the first time
again.
To confide secrets
we have yet to discover.
To stretch fingers
towards a knowing which nudges
the soul.

Here is where we'll meet,
when time
disappears.
Where I first see my
Self
and gasp
with delight,
knowing deep down
we were here
all along.

TWENTY-EIGHT
I AM AMAZING BECAUSE…

Love is the great miracle cure. Loving ourselves works miracles in our lives.

LOUISE HAY

Do we dare to acknowledge our strengths? Do we dare to acknowledge our weaknesses?

Some religions or schools of thought discourage pride. I still remember one time when my sister came to visit. At the time my first husband and I were living in the beautiful woods of South Lake Tahoe.

Denise and I got to speculating on the nature of reality but our musing came to a screeching halt when she firmly insisted her guru "knew *everything* there is to know." I challenged this, pointing out if God created humans 'in His image,' and humans are still learning, then God must be too.

This logic seems sound to me. We are the universe in loving motion, an infinite consciousness exploring, discovering, and becoming itself *through* us. We are the universe dreaming itself awake.

The logic was not as apparent to my sister, and my statement was instantly rejected. She quickly insisted I should pen a letter to her guru who apparently would set me straight. The guru who knew everything was an Indian master of Sant Mat who went by the name of Charan Singh back in the early 80's. I took a piece of paper right then and wrote out my belief, just as I shared here. Denise took it upon herself to mail it, and a few weeks later I received a reply.

This Indian master scolded and berated me, telling me pride is the devil's tool. A surprisingly biblical admonishment from an Eastern Mystic. This actually took me aback. Despite my aversion to joining paths (being a fiercely independent thinker) I respected my sister's explorations, and because of her devotion to Charan Singh, I automatically respected him as well. What I expected was a measured response, thoughtful and intelligent. In my view, any guru worth his or her salt should have unshakeable objectivity and a keen ability to reason and speculate. This spiritual 'leader' revealed an uneasy truth.

Leaders depend on followers.

Differing points of view are not encouraged, and dissent is quickly shut down. This is a practice that is unfortunately prevalent in any group dependent on power based solely on self-proclaimed authority, rather than on reason.

Nevertheless, she persisted.

My views have expanded but not veered much from many of my original speculations. I still firmly believe that we are indeed constantly learning, along with the core of creation, whether we call this core All That Is, God or Goddess, the Universe, or Universal Consciousness. Whatever magical essence of consciousness exists within us is along for this sometimes challenging, always exhilarating ride. We are sparkling seeds planted deep within a fertile garden of vast potential. If a brilliant lilac dares to burst into a fragrant, vibrant bloom, why can't I? So today, encouraged and inspired by friends and life itself, I shall boldly declare I am amazing!

"*I Am Amazing Because...*"

I am amazing because I've been courageous enough to honestly assess my hard-won choices, my wandering thoughts, my consequential decisions, and face up to the unnerving scrutiny of my self. To honestly evaluate my failures, my stinging blunders, my thoughtless boasts, and my often humbling shortcomings and still move forward. To face my moments of bluster and casual arrogance where I thought my cleverness took precedence over kindness and encouragement. To acknowledge I will indeed learn and grow and stumble and rise, as will every soul on this earth. To recognize that all of us, together or believing we are alone, will learn...eventually.

I am courageous because knowing my failures and my faults, I still persist and will continue to trust in who I will be. I am courageous because I believe in love.

Today let me encourage you to take a bold leap. To consider deeply, to let yourself dare to acknowledge that you are amazing.

Consider the years and tears you've invested in your growth, in your rocky path to personhood. Do you recognize the immeasurable strength, the soaring courage, the audacious daring it's taken you to get this far? Here's to you, dear friend.

SUGGESTED FOCUS:

Take a bold leap now and finish this sentence, "I am amazing because..." Take this daring opportunity to describe yourself from the viewpoint of one who would cherish all of you, every smile along with every wrinkle. Write a tribute to your Self.

. . .

AFFIRMATION: I choose to celebrate myself.

REVIEW:

To expand this further, write out a list of qualities you admire most, characteristics you would love to perceive within yourself, if only you dared. Now's the time to take that loving challenge. Following is a beginning list of qualities of being. Do expand it as more ideas spring to mind.

_I am_...

Courageous, charismatic, kind, resilient, determined, magical, elegant, focused, graceful, creative, passionate, flexible, spontaneous, responsible, gracious, compassionate, self-aware, imaginative, focused, productive, purposeful, generous, thoughtful, open-minded, reflective, playful, adventurous, hopeful, strong.

_I am_...

Open to new experiences, willing to listen, able to change my point of view, comfortable with being silly, eager to try new things.

After you read through the abbreviated list above, read it again, emphasizing the "**_I am_**..." Pay close attention to every emotion that arises. If you hear an instant denial, examine that. Do you know other people who seem to fit that characteristic? Consider this to be an unacknowledged shadow aspect that can be cultivated in your life.

Now repeat your list with the words: **_I can be_**...

How does this feel? Does it inspire or challenge you?

Using your imagination, create a scenario where you incorporate any characteristic you admire. Let yourself flow into this one, feeling all the emotions that arise.

TWENTY-NINE
FALL IN LOVE WITH YOURSELF

Love yourself first and everything else falls into line. You really have to love yourself to get anything done in this world.

LUCILLE BALL

I've known so many who unconsciously chose to focus on bringing happiness to others while neglecting to offer the same pleasure and joy to themselves. People who offer compassion to many, while remaining stern and unforgiving with their own hearts.

I was one.

It seems I was about nineteen, living in Portland, Oregon when I first wandered into that antique store and spotted an exquisite vintage jewelry box. The mother of pearl inlay gleamed against black lacquer, and the soft red velvet begged to cradle someone's beloved trinkets. The sight took my breath away. I saved up to buy this precious treasure, but not for me, to offer up as a gift to a friend I loved.

This was a long-standing habit of mine. I would yearn for something magnificent but rather than buy it for myself, I'd save up my dollars and give it away. Deep down I never believed in my own worth, so instead I offered up what seemed to be rare treasures to everyone but myself.

In similar manner, I would strive to view misbehavior by others with compassion—to grasp that their hurtful choices were rooted in a foundation of pain or fear—while severely chastising myself for any infraction. I'd offer sympathy to others while denying it for myself. When I'd share with others that my father died when I was three, the first response people offered was usually, "I'm so sorry." I'd quickly brush aside their sympathy and say something like, "It was really harder for my mom, for my brother and sister because they *knew* him, and I barely remember."

I'd endlessly go over my mistakes—the words blurted out, the unconscious thoughtlessness, the times my desire to best someone or be clever meant I unwittingly hurt another. I beat myself up so many times, I felt haunted by the vision of who I *should* be rather than inspired by who I really was.

If someone complimented me, I'd brush it aside and hurriedly confess my faults or fears. All the while never hesitating to offer sincere praise and appreciation to those I loved. So to me everyone's pain or loss was greater than my own, and everyone else was worthy of beautiful gifts or compliments, but not me.

At first glance, this appears altruistic. After all, others tell us being selfless is *good* and focusing on your own needs is selfish.

I don't agree.

Being self-less is no healthier than being selfish. It's an

imbalance that in time invariably creates a pendulum swing in the opposite direction.

It's also unrealistic. Those who believe in selflessness are often atoning for hidden fears.

My hidden fear sprang from the core belief that I was not a good person. This belief had a firm foundation thanks to my mom's careless words. What child can believe they are good if they are unwanted?

The pendulum swings in one way or the other. We may develop the narcissistic need to be better than everyone else, unconsciously competing with or belittling anyone who threatens our self-esteem, or we fervently believe everyone else is better than us, so we seek out those who quite conveniently agree we aren't worth the time.

The latter is the direction we go when our self-esteem has not developed properly.

The unacknowledged need and completely healthy desire to love ourselves can become distorted. Through outer conditioning or beliefs adopted, we may become convinced self-love, self-appreciation is wrong. This creates a schism, a fragmentation within our psyche. We disown those bits of our being which make us uncomfortable and project them outward. We avoid looking at ourselves realistically. We overcompensate.

In some cases, we may bend over backwards to appear selfless. We may offer up endless praise or compliments. Or volunteer to take on thankless tasks with unrealistic expectations. We'll brush away our feelings, pretending they don't matter. Sometimes even unconsciously denigrating those who have healthy boundaries.

They're so selfish!

In order to heal and become whole, we need to recognize, embrace, and integrate all aspects of self. We can't authentically love others until we authentically love our Selves.

Which is why the first step in learning how to genuinely love another requires us to begin at home within our own hearts. We must fall in love with our own sometimes fragile, faltering, eager-to-please, hopeful, pining self.

How do we begin?

We give to our own hearts, the same sincere compassion, all-encompassing forgiveness, tender empathy, radiant love, deep-felt admiration, and unwavering respect we offer to those we love.

Can we be our own best friends?

Can we treat ourselves with the same courtesy, gentle understanding, steadfast support, and compassionate kindness we would offer a beloved friend?

An invaluable and essential step in our healing is to recognize we are under no obligation to give to anyone. Everyone is responsible for their own well being. This may be a tremendous challenge but with the greatest compensation, not just for our own Selves but for those we love.

Why?

Because when we release ourselves from artificially constructed guilt (whether self-imposed or imposed on us by others) we are free to choose to give from our hearts, not from obligation. Without guilt or obligation, we give because it brings us pleasure, rather than providing a temporary bandage to a wound that never heals.

I'm giving because I want to, not because I have to. I choose to give when it feels right.

Choice is a beautiful thing. When we recognize choice, we empower ourselves. We also free others from the burden of feeling obligated to us in turn. A funny thing happens then. Giving feels good. Really good. Like an uplifting burst of pure love. A breath of pleasure as heady as life-giving oxygen.

Whether we're offering compassion or assistance, we can do

so recognizing there is no obligation. The person who receives then does not owe us a return favor.

There is no guilt.

We find giving makes us smile.

We no longer need to wonder if others appreciate us because we develop an honest appreciation for ourselves. We can then love freely, give generously without the underlying obligation which used to tug at our soul.

Another insight bubbles up. We notice others feel more relaxed around us when there is no obligation. The smiles we offer are freely returned. We notice how complimenting a stranger seems to brighten their mood, and the smiles continue to grow.

We begin by giving ourselves freedom to be ourselves. We begin by being compassionate and loving and appreciative and respectful with our own self. Within each of us is a soul as innocent and hopeful and joyous as a toddler twirling on a summer day. Let's remember to offer our inner selves the space, the love, and the trust necessary to explore, discover, and become fully the Self we most yearn to be.

Fall in love with yourself and watch her grow.

When I was a child, like many others, I yearned for love. I chased those who treated me with disrespect and threw myself into hurtful situations. My first boyfriend reflected back to me the low opinion I had for myself. He once said, "You're lucky that I love you because no-one else could love an ugly bitch like you."

Even now I shudder with pity for the broken shell of a being who could believe that was actually love. Every fear I clutched was thrown back at me with dagger-like precision. It took many years before I could honestly embrace the self-questioning vital for anyone reconstructing their self-esteem.

Why are we drawn to those who don't love us? What is it that we are trying to tell ourselves?

Why doesn't he love me?

Why don't I love myself?

Reality faithfully reflects our beliefs back so that we can see in bitter detail what we shrink away from acknowledging. It provides a mirror, which can help us perceive the truths that we're not quite ready to hear. It whispers, *Do you rage at a universe that doesn't provide love, while you withhold love from your Self? Do you demand proof of your worth, while treating your beloved self as worthless?* Many of us seek a respite from the nagging fear that we have yet to understand—that we must always love ourselves first.

When we begin an authentic practice of self-love, the world responds in kind. When we embrace the truest relationship we will ever have—the enduring love story between soul and self—we will no longer need to chase shadows. We will no longer wonder when love will find us, for we will have found love. The sweet breath of kindness, compassion, and adoration we seek is nestled within our own hearts. Offer up this appreciation to the one who needs you most, the one who will be with you from first to last breath. Fall in love with your Self.

SUGGESTED FOCUS:

Authentic self-love is the goal and yet for some of us, the goal seems out of reach. How do we 'fall in love' with our Self?

The tried and true exercise of gazing in the mirror is always recommended for one reason. It works. When a parent nurses a child, she or he gazes deeply into baby's eyes. When we first meet and fall in love, we share hopes and secrets while connecting with our eyes.

In every love story, there's a beginning.

Mirror Connection:

Step one. Find a comfortable space where you can feel free to stare into a mirror for at least five minutes. If standing for that length of time is a challenge, pull up a chair or utilize a hand mirror.

Step two. First off, declare your love sincerely. At first this can feel awkward or uncomfortable. **"I love you."** Consider each bruise on your soul, every scar that tugs at your heart. Be gentle, as if this self in the mirror were an abused child you are convincing or a feral pet that's been abandoned and is uncertain whether it's safe to trust again. **"I love you."**

Step three. At this point, your inner child may begin to squirm and wonder. Answer that unspoken question, "Why do you love me?" Respond to her or him. Point out your best qualities, recount the struggles you've overcome, convince your Soul she or he is worthy of love.

First Date:

Sometimes awkward yet always memorable is when we flow into that first date. You are now in the process of both wooing and getting to know your Self. Even better, you can choose exactly the date that would please you most. What aspect of self needs attention first? How would you woo yourself?

Imagine that you can plan your perfect day/evening. Get a piece of paper and write down your most spectacular first date. Politely show "realistic" the door and instead jot down every single lavish idea that pops into mind.

Being flown to Italy for dinner by a private chef in Tuscany?
Chauffeured to an award-winning restaurant?
Having flowers delivered with a love note?
A picnic by a river with all your favorite foods?
Going hiking to a pristine lake?
A movie night followed by a tasty dessert?

Going dancing or soaking in a scented bath with flower petals?

A spa day?

As you write these ideas down, imagine yourself doing each one. Feel the pleasure and exhilaration. While you do this repeat these words: "I'd give all this to you and more because <u>you are worth it</u>."

Follow-up by choosing an activity that appeals to you specifically. If you're the one who 'gives in' for the sake of harmony, it's even more vital to choose a "me only" date. Once you've made your plans, write down a love note to yourself to place in a sealed envelope. If you can, pick yourself up a small gift, a token to remember your first date. Since you know what You love, this can be a fun project.

The night before your first date, set out the gift and love note. Prepare for your date exactly as pleases you. If you want to dress up and style your hair, do that. If you'd rather slip on your most comfy clothes sans make-up, do that. Before you begin your date, open your gift and read the accompanying letter.

Make this the first of many personal dates with your Self, because you are worth it!

AFFIRMATION: <u>I am a wonderful being, a soul who is worthy of love and respect. Today I choose me.</u>

REVIEW:

Our review will integrate our release of obligation and our new practice of self-love.

Picture a situation in which you feel obligation, whether that obligation is to do a task or act in a certain way. Now say, "<u>I Choose To...</u>"

How does that feel? Is it actually a choice or instead are you feeling obligated?

When we actually want to do a task, like providing a tasty meal for our enthusiastic puppy or brushing the hair of our squirmy toddler, we are choosing. Even in those moments when time or temper is short, we would make this choice.

Tasks that are thrust upon us (like the example I offered early on with Ross and Phoebe, "I wish I could, but I don't want to...") are a great example of obligation.

"I Choose to Feel Obligated to Help Ross Move." Except she didn't.

It's time to take the bold step and consider... what if I can choose to not feel obligated?

Note to self—as of today, I will remember: <u>*everyone is responsible for their own wellbeing. I always have the power of choice.*</u>

Now let's follow up with self-love.

How often when we glance in the mirror do we note our imperfections? Just as we did with our mirror connection exercise, let's make it a practice to be our own best friend. If you hear any negative self-talk arise, counter it with a loving affirmation. Point out the best attributes and offer reassurance to your fears. Try to consciously remember to do this for at least one month, or until you find this to be an automatic choice.

"I love you!" "You are incredible!" "You rocked that presentation!" "You're always so capable!" "You are an artist!"

<u>*Love notes:*</u>

Once a week, write yourself a love note (you can type it or handwrite, whichever feels comfortable) and read it to yourself the next day. Note your accomplishments of the week, reflect on your growth, point out at least one fabulous choice that brought you pleasure.

Save each and every note in a dedicated box. These love

letters will continue to inspire you throughout your life. If you are craft-oriented, create a special box where they can be stored. Even an old shoebox can be covered with stickers, favorite sayings, or old photos.

Every day for a month, come up with one positive affirmation that uplifts you. If creating your own affirmations presents a challenge, feel free to search them out online or be inspired by notable authors like Louise Hay or Marianne Williamson.

Be sure to write those affirmations down and put them in your love-letter box.

If time permits (and it's a good idea to carve out a few hours weekly), make the 'date-night' (or day) a regular weekly practice. Even once a month can be rejuvenating. Keep souvenirs of every date. A ticket-stub, a photo, a take-out menu, a memento. All should be stored in your love-letter box.

Special Project:

Get some paper and cut fifty-two long strips. On each strip, write an abbreviated love note to yourself. Point out your best qualities, offer encouragement, remind yourself of an accomplishment, or write down an affirmation that makes your heart sing.

Roll each paper up and tie it with a ribbon. Put these love notes into a jar. At the beginning of every week, pull one out and read it to yourself.

THIRTY
THE UNFINISHED PORTRAIT

Trust dreams. Trust your heart, and trust your story.

NEIL GAIMAN

Reality is an inspiring, incredible, and sometimes frustrating classroom. It's been cathartic and illuminating to recognize, in retrospect, how every piece of my life fits together so neatly. No matter how many times I've been brought to my knees, or broken down in bitter tears facing my inadequacies (or what appears at the time to be gross injustices), my reflections always nudge me to perceive the kernel of wisdom hidden within.

Even as I struggled through the edits, and my fingers typed up each chapter, lessons arose as I grappled with fears and examined my worry that being an eternal student automatically disqualifies me from believing I have any insight to offer. Maybe yes, maybe no. What is undeniably true is this.

We are *all* teachers as well as eternal students.

Every circumstance, every struggle and triumph is a lesson

from which we can glean wisdom. We don't need starkly dramatic events or to be swept up by a tornado in order to discover the value of finding our way home to our selves. The fictional Dorothy of Oz inspired me but I have neither need nor desire to slay witches or battle fierce opponents in order to be my own heroic self. It is the values of these mythical heroes I yearn to embrace, not the horrific circumstances, and those values can and should be acquired and integrated in the most commonplace moments as well as the extraordinary days of our lives.

My stories are sometimes quite ordinary because life itself is not meant to be a constant struggle. Wisdom doesn't rely on crisis and no, we don't require suffering in order to appreciate happiness.

My understanding has unfolded over the decades my feet have trod upon this earth, and will continue to expand until my last breath. I expect to constantly question and review my life, my choices, and even my self, because my portrait will remain unfinished until my life is done.

What I do know, and will take with me into my next incarnation, is the wisdom and insight I've garnered, not the memory of specific incidents.

We choose every circumstance in order to learn.

Books like *The Secret* and even as far back as Napoleon Hill's classic, *Think and Grow Rich*, will tell you, quite rightly, that what you focus on will be brought forth into your life. Yet this reality is not simply a paint-by-number set where you merely have to select the right colors and suddenly everything will be fabulous.

There's a great song by Rod Stewart called, "Every Picture Tells a Story." That title pretty much sums up a lovely esoteric concept. We are living portraits composed of stories. What we're meant to do with every action and interaction, every choice and every result, is to learn from the stories we encounter, and even more importantly, the stories we tell with every word and every choice.

We are all meant to become the best possible person a soul could be. To choose kindness over thoughtlessness; to help, not hurt; to recognize that our thoughts, attitudes, and emotions are reflected back to us in countless ways.

Twenty years or so ago, I had traveled to visit one of my friends. Nighttime rolled around and I curled up in the guest room with a good book. My hostess popped by to say goodnight. This was an old friend who I'll call Sally. Anyway, as we chatted a bit, Sally's cat padded over and then paused at the doorjamb, quizzically glancing my way but with obvious hesitation.

I called over to the sweet kitty but still she lingered uncertainly, pausing to glance up at Sally who said, "It's okay, you can go say hi, I won't be jealous."

The words sent a shockwave through me.

Wow, I thought to myself, *that's not how I see it at all.*

The contrast rattled me. My thoughts would more likely be, "It's okay—she won't hurt you."

That was the difference between us.

We were both projecting our beliefs onto the cat, when truly we had no idea what the kitty was really thinking. My friend though did have serious issues with control and would adamantly share how she simply never felt jealous. Yet it was the first thing that popped into her mind.

Me?

Clearly my issue was about safety, and more specifically, vulnerability.

My focus would be to reassure the sweet cat that *she'd* be okay.

My friend's perspective was that the cat was worried about *her* feelings instead.

This ordinary moment is just one of many, and all of them can teach us if we are willing to notice, and courageous enough to reflect.

What is this moment telling me?

If we believe the only truly meaningful lessons are those that are hard-won, then that is what we will seek and that is what we will find. If we believe wisdom can be found by recognizing that our own attitudes, beliefs, and patterns are reflected back in even the most ordinary of days, that is what we will find.

It is in the everyday moment that we live. It is there we discover who we truly are. It is within this eternal moment that we live.

You and me, we're walking this path together.

Together we will find our way home.

THIRTY-ONE
OUR WAY HOME

Love is a whisper
of reassurance.
Guilt a stabbing
breath of fear that I don't
belong.
The promise of love offered
a corner
for my soul to turn around.

Self-acceptance meant transforming
mirrors of doubt,
owning what scared me
most.
Vulnerability
taught me.

Those moments of
passion and clarity
flashed,
a lightning bolt shattering
dusky windows where I gazed
still hopeful
love would rescue
me.

I learned to trust,
forgive,
accept each
heartbreaking reveal
without turning away from my
Self.

Ordinary me
is extraordinary.
No need to battle
mythic dragons whose words
singe like cold fire.
I am
enough.

I learned to give.

Smiles to strangers with weary faces,
doors held open in life and in
heart.
Just a quick glance, a soft smile
to let another know
she's not alone.

One heart candle lights
another, through acts so
commonplace
we forget everyday heroes
don't need capes.

Grab a hunk of goodwill to toss
on that bonfire of crackling
good intentions.
Taking a fraction of a second to
remember,
heals our fear
of being.

Love arrived
not on an imaginary stallion
offering a dashing
prince
and a fairytale castle in the sky.
Love did rescue me
from the fear of not seeing
my truth.

The mirror and I are one.

Reflections every
where:
in others
singing
an unspoken tune,
a majestic leaf
dancing,
a dragonfly daring
to test new wings,
or
a shy flush of self-love
when we peek
behind the curtain
and
in a flash of intimate
knowing,
realize
we have found our way
home.

ACKNOWLEDGMENTS

George, without you this book couldn't exist. Thank you for pushing me off the dock and then jumping in when the current got rough. Your endless (okay, maybe not endless but damn close) patience with round after round of edits, and your painstaking research on the various details of publication brought this book to life. Plus you rock that electric guitar on Saturday's music night, which is the most delicious fuel for my inner fire.

Everyone needs someone generous enough to examine a new project, and for me that would be my Beta Readers: Elizabeth Cody, Brenda Bowen, Kirby Miller, and Kris Kachirisky. Thank you for making the time to peruse the draft I sincerely thought was the final. You handled me with gentle kindness while also helping me to perceive the potential within my book. Special thanks to Beth for introducing me to my first editor, Alice Anderson, who highlighted the missing pieces throughout my manuscript. We can't improve something without seeing what's required. Alice, I am grateful for your diligence and encouragement.

Extraordinary women like my chosen sisters, Cathy Simmons, Carla Holmes, Brenda Bowen, and Misty Evans, are the lifeblood of a soul family. You four have seen me through the rockiest of times and metaphorically held my hand whenever tears tumbled out, and you always cheer me on when I need it most. You rock my world. Thanks, sisters.

Finally, despite the criticism of social media, many of my closest friends and cohorts are found there. Too numerous to list, but please know that your encouragement and appreciation of my words are why this book came to be. To my beautiful friends and followers on Facebook, thank you.

ABOUT THE AUTHOR

Chiron O'Keefe is a poet, writer and the author of *Bravely You, Bravely Me: Being You Without Apology,* her first non-fiction book. Woven together by the major themes of her life story, each chapter provides insight and inspiration to those seeking a sense of self within a fragmented world.

    She resides with her husband in Oregon, and is currently working on her second non-fiction book. You can follow Chiron on Facebook, Twitter, and Instagram, or at chironokeefe.com

    facebook.com/chironokeefe

    twitter.com/chironokeefe

    instagram.com/chironokeefe

Made in United States
North Haven, CT
03 May 2022